The
Supply Chain
Network
@
Internet Speed

The
Supply Chain
Network
@
Internet Speed

Preparing Your Company
for the
E-Commerce Revolution

Fred A. Kuglin
Barbara A. Rosenbaum

AMACOM
American Management Association

New York • Atlanta • Boston • Chicago • Kansas City • San Francisco • Washington, D. C.
Brussels • Mexico City • Tokyo • Toronto

This publication is designed to provide accurate and authoritative information in regard to the subject matter covered. It is sold with the understanding that the publisher is not engaged in rendering legal, accounting, or other professional service. If legal advice or other expert assistance is required, the services of a competent professional person should be sought.

Library of Congress Cataloging-in-Publication Data

Kuglin, Fred A.
    The Supply Chain network @ Internet speed : preparing your company for the E-commerce revolution / Fred A. Kuglin, Barbara A. Rosenbaum.
        p.   cm.
    Includes bibliographical references and index.
    ISBN 0-8144-0595-9
    1. Industrial procurement.   2. Electronic commerce.   3. Internet.
I. Rosenbaum, Barbara A.   II. Title.

HD39.5 .K83 2000
658.8'4—dc21   00–044803

Printing number

10 9 8 7 6 5 4 3 2 1

CONTENTS

LIST OF

EXHIBITS

INTRODUCTION

The Changing World of Supply Chain Management

LEADERSHIP AND CHANGE

Several months ago, representatives of the World Economic Forum assembled in a major South American city for one of their conferences. Many top political and economic leaders attended the conference as well. The focus of many discussions at the conference was on the Internet, in particular on how it was changing the global economy.

Many informal discussions were also held by smaller groups of attendees, one of which centered on the critical factors necessary for countries and companies to thrive in the Internet economy during the next five to ten years. The input from the participants varied according to the number of countries involved in the discussion.

However, there were a couple of points that everyone agreed were essential:

- Sooner or later, companies involved with the Internet will have to produce shareholder value through results. (The NASDAQ response in April 2000 supported this point.)
- The CEO's job description has changed to one of leadership through technology-driven transformation.
- The use of the Internet has exponentially increased the complexities—and opportunities—involving the supply chain.
- The changes being driven by technology and the Internet are creating a need for top management to understand both their industries *and* technology.

⊕ The leadership in applying technology and using the Internet in e-commerce and e-business will most likely come from the United States.

The discussions were often spirited but healthy. The group's energy showed a high level of optimism for the new Internet-based global economy. One extremely successful man in his seventies summed up this optimism for the whole group. He said:

> I wish I was a young man again and just starting my career. There is more opportunity in the world right now than there ever has been in my lifetime. We are creating a new economy where industries, supply chains, and services are blurring together. We will have new winners and losers, with the winners learning and changing every day. I wonder if I could achieve the same success in moving forward that I have achieved in the last forty years!

These were very profound and humble words from someone who is a self-made billionaire. However, his message about opportunity, learning, and change rang true with everyone present.

This book is about leadership through transformation. It is written in a day-in-the-life-of-a-CEO format. Each chapter focuses on a particular industry and a mythical chief executive officer (CEO) of a major company. The scenarios interspersed throughout the chapters are an aid in understanding the current state of each industry and the potential technology-driven transformation solutions for solving specific industry problems. Each chapter highlights a specific intelligent e-business solution, as depicted in Exhibit I-1, and one of the five drivers of shareholder value, as depicted in Exhibit I-2.

The outline of the book is as follows:

Chapter Value	Industry	E-Business Solution	Shareholder Driver
One	General Mfg./ Introduction	War Room	Overview
Two	Retail/ Consumer Products	Web-Based Catalogs, Scan-Based Trading	Profitable Growth
Three	High-Tech	Networked Supply Chain, HightechMatrix™	Working-Capital Mini-mization
Four	Automotive	Trade E-Exchanges	Fixed-Capital Minimization
Five	Oil & Gas	E-Exchange Spare Parts	Cost Minimiza-tion
Six	Transportation	.comLLPs	Tax Minimiza-tion
Seven	Health Care	Product Life Management	Fixed-Asset Minimization
Eight	Internet Speed	TradeMatrix™ Straight Eights	All-Summary
Nine	The Next Wave of Supply Chain Value and Dean of IT Supply Chain Management		

THE POWER OF CHANGE

The successful man who spoke so eloquently to our group in South America also spoke to a small group of us at the end of the conference. He asked if we really understood how quickly change was occurring in the world. He then asked if we knew who the top technology or what the top industrial companies around the world were in 1990. He then asked everyone if, ten years ago, we had envisioned the Internet, or purchasing

(text continues on page xx)

Exhibit I-1. Intelligent e-business solutions.

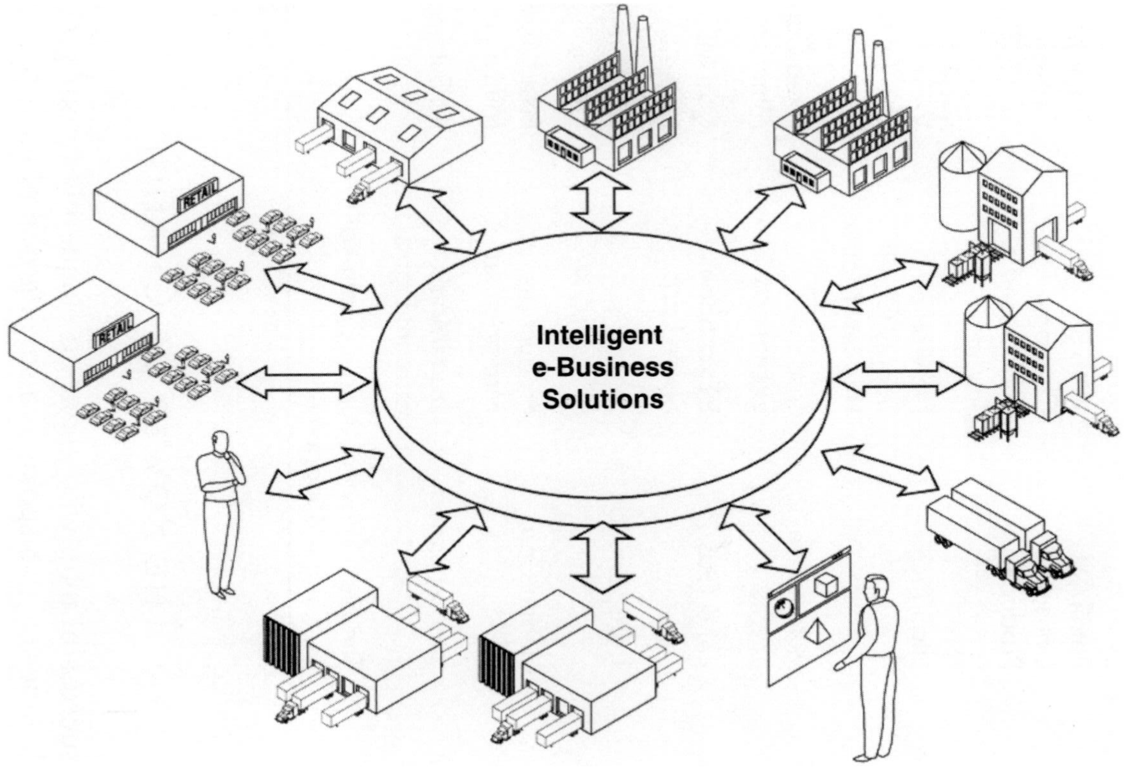

Source: i2 Technologies.

Exhibit I-2. The five drivers of shareholder value.

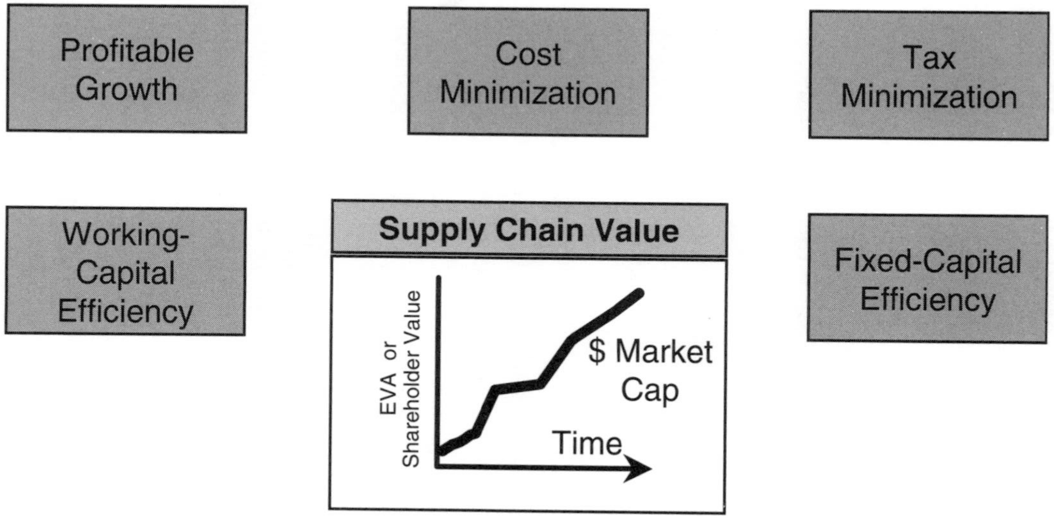

Profitable Growth	Cost Minimization	Tax Minimization

Working-Capital Efficiency		Fixed-Capital Efficiency

Supply Chain Value

EVA or Shareholder Value

$ Market Cap

Time

Source: Cap Gemini Ernst & Young.

e-exchanges, e-marketplaces, or 24 × 7 on-line global design of electronics and automobiles from Web sites around the world, or blurring supply chains as companies enter one another's industries?

This man's parting message was for us to appreciate and understand the challenges facing the CEOs of Global 1000 companies. Many of these CEOs advanced in their companies during the pre-Internet era. However, Wall Street is now pounding on their doors and demanding that they develop a plan to mutate their companies into *.com*panies. For many CEOs, this represents a challenge they have never been prepared to address.

CONCLUSION

The technology-driven changes in the global economy are providing opportunities and threats to everyone, including CEOs. The changes are so pervasive that traditional industry and competitor models are being disassembled at Internet speed. One of the worst options is to do nothing, because your competitors are trying everything.

The wise man at the recent high-tech conference told a funny joke with serious underpinnings. He said that if you believed that an "exchange" was something involving your telephone company, you were in big trouble. He explained that telephone operators once helped people navigate the myriad of telephone exchanges. He then challenged the group to thoroughly understand what Internet-driven exchanges are and to seek out their own "exchange operators" from inside or outside their companies. He finished his joke by telling everyone that life will be a nonstop busy signal for those who do not adopt technology-driven transformation as part of their go-forward strategies.

ACKNOWLEDGMENTS

FROM

FRED A. KUGLIN

This book was inspired by my shared passion with Sanjiv Sidhu and Ken Sharma for changing the way the world does business. It is intended to follow the spirit of the original PLANET conferences, which was dedicated to the vision of achieving a new paradigm for supply chain management through the effective use of technology.

I want to thank my wife and children for their patience, support, and understanding throughout the writing process. In addition, I want to thank Chris Gopal and Fred Crawford for sharing with me the passion to write and the support to make this book a reality. Also, I want to thank Hiten Varia of i2 Technologies, and Barbara Rosenbaum, my coauthor, for their support and contributions to this book. Special thanks go to Mark Finlayson of i2 Technologies and his fine support of the Cap Gemini Ernst & Young Alliance with i2 Technologies.

In addition, I want to thank Dr. Les Waters for his continued support and inspiration. Special thanks also go to Tom Gunn, Steve Johnson, and Bruce Bone for their friendship and encouragement to pursue supply chain excellence in our ever-changing world.

Lastly, I want to thank my parents for giving me the encouragement to reach out for objectives originally thought to be out of reach, and the discipline to work the hours necessary to achieve these objectives.

ACKNOWLEDGMENTS

FROM

BARBARA A.

ROSENBAUM

First, my thanks go to Fred Kuglin for initiating the concept for this book and inviting me to join him as the coauthor. It has been a pleasure to work with Fred over the course of this project, as we have shared a vision as to the dramatic changes taking place in supply chain management due to the use of technology and the Internet.

Secondly, my thanks go to the supply chain practice of Cap Gemini Ernst & Young under the leadership of Phil Robers. The practice has developed a clear, innovative vision for the supply chain network in the Internet economy. In particular, I would like to thank Kevin O'Laughlin, Chap Kistler, Rich Behling, La Verne Council, Al Montgomery, Rich Thompson, Wendy Burke, Howard Kirssin, Amy Reed, Lydon Neumann, Mark Van Sumeren, Bill Shriver, Kevin Poole, and Tom Tretter for their review and assistance in crafting the book's message.

Additionally, my thanks go to Gene Tyndall, a former colleague and friend, of Ryder System, Inc., for his thoughts and direction, and to Jim Godbout, Guy Sanschagrin, Mark Claybon, and Michael Mimbs of Ernst & Young LLP, for their insights on tax-effective supply chain management.

Finally, my thanks go to my husband, Henry, my children, Ted and Paulina, and to my mother, Frieda, for their love and support for all of my endeavors.

The
Supply Chain
Network
@
Internet Speed

1

THE CEO'S
DECISION

*Creating Opportunity
out of Crisis*

INTRODUCTION

The CEO of a major manufacturing company had just returned to the United States from a trip to the Far East and South America. As he settled into his favorite chair on the deck of his lake house near Austin, Texas, he reflected on the discoveries of his trip. Despite a continuing financial crisis in the Far East, he found the people in many countries there to be educated, adept at using technology, and willing to work in a pay-for-performance environment. In addition, he found a significant population base of potential consumers who had a pent-up demand for products like those that his company produces.

In South America, he found that the democracies in Chile, Argentina, and Brazil were growing stronger despite the severe devaluation of the Brazilian *real.* The CEO also found a growing population in Brazil that was educated and adept at using technology, despite an illiteracy rate of 15 to 17 percent. He was especially impressed with the city of Campinas, which is located approximately eighty kilometers northeast of São Paulo. Campinas is home to several high-tech manufacturing and assembly operations and to a major university. Because of its relative political, social, and economic stability, the CEO concluded that the Mercosur trading bloc held long-term promise despite recent troubles with the Brazilian economy.

As he watched a fisherman catch a fish off the shore from his lake house, the CEO's thoughts turned to his own company. The current profit picture was positive. Demand for his company's products had steadily increased sales by approximately 10 percent per year for the past five years. Earnings before interest, depreciation, and amortization (EBIDA) had increased 15 + percent during the same period, fueled primarily by lower commodity prices. The company's investment in its fixed-asset base had declined during the past five years, but was about to increase because of the replacement cycle of some key manufacturing equipment and the building of a new plant to expand capacity. Inventory turnover was a stubborn problem because of the buying cycles of customers and the hedge-buying of commodities by his purchasing department. Receivables were high, and had been for the past five years. To combat inventory turnover and receivables' impact on cash flow, his company delayed paying its suppliers for up to eighty days. The CEO knew that his actions would have a long-term impact on his purchased materials' cost, but it was helping to alleviate his cash-flow problem in the short term.

Just then, the telephone rang. The chief financial officer (CFO) was calling to inform the CEO that the company had just experienced a fire at one of its major manufacturing sites in North Carolina. Fortunately, the fire occurred early on a Saturday morning just before the first shift, and no one was hurt. However, early estimates were that over 50 percent of the plant had been destroyed, and production would be halted for approximately six months. The CEO knew that he had to act fast. The security analysts would be calling to know the impact on earnings and to be reassured that he was in control. The employees would want to know how they would be impacted from an employment standpoint. In addition, there were his customers, many of whom had long-term relationships with his company. The CEO told the CFO to request the use of the "war room" on an emergency basis.

THE WAR ROOM

The war room uses an accelerated solutions environment (ASE) that provides technology and services to perform business-process optimization and scenario-planning that take hours, not months, to complete. This facility, as shown in Exhibit 1-1, uses intelligent e-business technologies to calculate

Exhibit 1-1. Accelerated solutions environment and the war room.

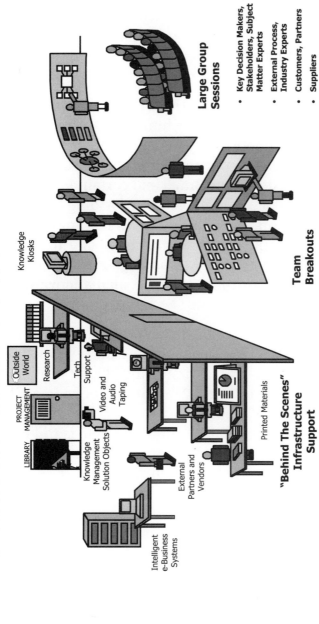

Source: Cap Gemini Ernst & Young.

the collaborative impact of changes in demand on supply planning, factory planning, and supply chain planning. The results tie into a series of *pro forma* financial reports, including P&Ls and balance sheets. The disruption in demand due to the factory fire could be quickly modeled and the results reproduced in a form that could be communicated to the board of directors and security analysts.

After making a series of telephone calls to arrange for the emergency use of the ASE, the CEO again reflected on his recent trip. It then dawned on him. This unfortunate plant fire may provide an opportunity to restructure his company to take advantage of other opportunities in the marketplace. The time to invest seemed right in Brazil and certain Far East countries. The emergence of e-commerce was providing his company with both an opportunity and a threat. Since times were good, the CEO did not want to disrupt his company to bet on such a small market—despite the prodding of Wall Street analysts. However, the opportunity to make such a move was now presenting itself.

The CEO also recalled the eight success principles for dealing with Wall Street concerning an operational crisis, as listed in Exhibit 1-2. The first principle for dealing with Wall Street is to "Be prepared." Wall Street looks to a CEO for answers, and the CEO must provide a defined timetable in which to get these answers. The second principle is to "Be principle-centered." Wall Street looks for consistency in performance. It does not like inconsistencies in the value base during times of stress, which could translate into inconsistencies in future financial performance. The third principle is to "Be fact-based." Facts are what they are, but opinions are open to interpretation and should be avoided whenever possible. Stick with the facts, and categorize them into one of three groups: situation, complication, and solution. The fourth principle is to "Be honest." Dishonesty breeds distrust, and will exponentially increase the complexity of the crisis. In addition, the CEO will be forever questioned by Wall Street if dishonesty is ever exhib-

Exhibit 1-2. Eight crisis principles for the CEO: dealing with Wall Street during an operational crisis.

1. *Be prepared.* Wall Street is looking to the CEO to be in control and to communicate quickly. If you do not have the answers right away, then have a plan to get the answers and communicate that plan to Wall Street.

2. *Be principle-centered.* Wall Street looks for the go-forward plan that extends a company's vision and value base. This anchor represents stability, which also translates into consistency of performance against expectations.

3. *Be fact-based.* The best approach is to describe events in three groupings: situation, complications, and solutions. Do not render opinions without knowing the facts.

4. *Be honest.* Dishonesty breeds distrust. The crisis "mountain" to climb increases exponentially when dishonesty is introduced into the equation.

5. *Be accessible.* Security analysts usually greet absence and silence during a time of crisis with high skepticism. Schedule regular conference calls and answer messages from analysts on a timely basis.

6. *Be emphathetic.* Analysts have jobs to do, and have a number of investors counting on their opinions and intuitions. Pressure is on them, just as it is on the CEO, the employees, the suppliers, and the communities that are affected by the crisis. Real people have real feelings, so demonstrate sensitivity to those feelings.

7. *Be patient.* Avoid losing patience or displaying irritability during conference calls or discussions. If you lose your patience, you will be reminded of your slip in the stock price and through the analysts' reports.

8. *Be yourself.* Avoid trying to be someone different to analysts during a time of crisis.

Source: Fred A. Kuglin, Cap Gemini Ernst & Young.

ited. The fifth principle is to "Be accessible." Security analysts usually greet absence and silence during a time of crisis with high skepticism. The security analysts are pressured by their stockholders for information and answers. It is acceptable to discuss limited facts, and the process for future discovery of additional facts. Limited knowledge is better than the absence of knowledge. The sixth principle is to "Be empathetic." Analysts have jobs to do. They have many investors counting on their opinions and intuitions. The pressure is on them, just as it is on the CEO, the employees, the suppliers, and the communities affected. Real people have real feelings, so demonstrate sensitivity to these feelings. The seventh principle is to "Be patient." The CEO must be in control. Security analysts will correlate a loss of emotional control with a lack of organizational control. Being calm during a crisis will help the CEO enlist the urgent support needed to lead the company out of its crisis. The eighth and last principle is to "Be yourself." Once again, security analysts look for and reward consistency. Part of their investment opinion for a company's stock is their knowledge, understanding, and belief in the CEO. Any major surprise in this principle usually marks the beginning of the end for the CEO as far as Wall Street is concerned.

Our CEO vowed to himself that he would be prepared and follow the eight success principles for dealing with Wall Street concerning an operational crisis. He also knew that he had to answer several questions. How could he quickly stabilize his current operations and make the decisions necessary for investing globally and in e-commerce? How could he ensure that his executive staff was aligned with this new company vision and supportive of the restructuring steps during this crisis? How could he pull all of this together in a plan that would signal Wall Street, his customers, and his employees that he was in control? How could he be assured that all of his actions supported the primary drivers of shareholder value? He knew that he needed to put these questions on the table when he discussed the situation with his senior staff the next morning.

THE WAR ROOM

Sunday, 3:00 P.M.:
Crisis Response and Strategy Development

Preparation

After the CEO placed his call to reserve the war room, the team assembled for the war room exercise. The senior management group and its staff of approximately twenty-five people arrived at the war room on a Sunday afternoon. At check-in, they each received a package detailing several items to provide a common base of understanding for the group. This package contained

- A description of the unfolding crisis and the CEO's vision of creating opportunity from the crisis
- A request for immediate data to be sent on-line to the war room team
- Templates to be filled in with on-line data that provides a breakdown of the company's products, markets, geographies, and operations in terms of costs, margins, and capacity structures. Included in this on-line data request are:

  —Current orders unfilled by the North Carolina plant fire

  —Costs per product and channel for each stage of their supply chain, broken down by assets, people (direct and indirect), overhead, and material (direct and indirect)

  —An outline of their key customers by channel and the cost-to-serve for each

—Working capital by type and stage

—A profile of new products introduced, including number, type, sales, and margins

—Their investment in fixed assets and a profile of their physical network

—The demand/supply constraints that support their physical network

⊕ A compilation of secondary research on consumer buying patterns, channel and industry trends and dynamics by various geographies, including South America and selected Far East countries

⊕ A competitive industry profile on selected and key metrics, including the best in other industries

⊕ The five drivers of shareholder value that must anchor the end product of the war room exercise

The security and sensitivity around the war room exercise were intense. Each page of the briefing reports was an original (with the word "original" stamped in red ink and numbered with the code of the participant so that copying would be discouraged). The data was then sent on-line to the war room, and the templates were completed.

The group was asked to spend the afternoon in small interfunctional groups of five people each in breakout rooms, making notes and drawing conclusions across several dimensions that were provided. In each group, data and process experts facilitated the discussion. Each group was provided with one notebook computer with preset templates on which to save their answers on disk.

The CEO spent Sunday evening huddled with his senior staff discussing operational options and travel logistics for the upcoming week. The senior staff appeared exhausted, and the week was only beginning. The CEO reiterated his desire to secure the answers to his stated questions. This whole process would need to produce answers or it would be a failure.

Monday, 8:00 A.M.:
In the War Room—it looked like a testosterone-soaked accelerated solutions environment (ASE) and operated like one.

Scenarios and Quick Crisis-Response Actions

The war room group was provided with an introduction to the session's objectives, the company's financial and market objectives (obtained earlier from the CEO), and the process and ground rules. Then each group was asked to present its conclusions from the previous afternoon. They presented their questions and views as follows:

- What must be done immediately to allocate customer demand to other plant/logistics centers to protect their customers' orders? What is the impact on their customers (order fill rates, delivery times, etc.), their employees (overtime, loss of work or displacement of work, etc.), and their business (sales, earnings, CapEx spending, etc.)?
- What is the current business model in North America, South America, Europe, and Asia/Pacific? (For example, How do they make money?, What are the key areas for cost reduction?, and What customer needs are they meeting or not meeting?)
- What do they perceive as the essential industry trends affecting them? What customer and consumer patterns of the future do they need to meet?
- What are the best practices that they have identified from the data?
- Is there any additional information needed to effectively answer these questions?

The presentations were displayed on large-screen monitors and immediately collated electronically. The senior executive team reviewed the short-term action plans before agreement was reached through a consensus-building exercise and the next steps were agreed to by all. Included in these steps was a prearranged conference call with key Wall Street security analysts to be held at noon. The critical path in this process involved speed. The CEO needed to be prepared for the security analysts, and the executive team needed to be prepared to execute. There was no time for "paralysis by analysis."

At the end of this phase, the collated set of results was printed out for each senior executive participant. This formed part of a binder that was added to during the next few days, providing a reference for each individual participant. Again, each set and each binder were originals, appropriately numbered and assigned. Strict controls needed to be in place to prevent leakage or corporate espionage. While the binders reflected the completed tasks being assembled, the war room knowledge workers were simultaneously researching additional necessary information.

After the short-term crisis plan was drafted, the group split up into functional groups. They then attended a session to craft different functional scenarios (operations, marketing/new products, sales, information systems) that included what could be done differently under a variety of market, cost, and competitive challenges. They used models for impact analysis that had been constructed earlier by the joint team using best-in-class software, as shown in Exhibit 1-3. These models were captured electronically and displayed in both the group work area and on the big-screen monitors in the radiant room. Every scenario, captured electronically, was printed out immediately for each participant in an original, numbered format.

The whole group then got back together in the radiant room and was led through a discussion of strategic intent and ideas (new markets, new products, and new operational models). All work was captured and displayed electronically. This "enterprise-wide scenario generation" session directly generated potential scenarios based on the group discussion. Agreement and consensus on the potential scenarios were secured before the group left the room.

Exhibit 1-3. Best-in-class software—sample.

War Room Software Tools
Supply Chain Strategist
Logistics Tools
Supply Chain Planner
Simulation Tools
Rapid APS Value Generator
Tax Evaluator
Shareholder Impact Tool
Others

The primary team then took a break to eat dinner. Meanwhile, facilitators, analysts, and knowledge workers aided by software advisors were busy modifying the models to reflect the new market and operational environment. This included impacts, cost flows, and, developed with the executive sponsor team, the challenges to the scenarios that had been developed earlier. The participants were then assigned to different groups based on function. They were facilitated in each session to develop immediate improvements within their own functions. The improvements were captured electronically and displayed both in the work area and on the big-screen monitors in the main radiant room. The participants saw the effects of their improvements on the financial picture via a model of their functional area, which had been developed earlier. (For each improvement, the group estimated an impact, a cost, and a period.)

Monday, 8:00 P.M.: Dinner

The primary team met with the CEO for dinner. The CEO appeared to be comfortable with the output from the day's events and the response from the security analysts. At the end of dinner, he placed a challenge before the group. How could the primary team address the e-commerce strategy of the company while developing a rapid response program at the same time? As shown in Exhibit 1-4, the e-business, or business-to-business side of e-commerce, is booming, and the savings are immense. The CEO not only wanted to respond strongly to Wall Street, but he wanted to dazzle them during the next couple of conference calls.

The primary team was now not only exhausted but a little overwhelmed at this request. They had to now shift their thinking from fulfilling actual open customer orders to the development of an e-commerce strategy. They retired for the evening, knowing that a good night's rest would help them think through this recent request.

Tuesday, 8 A.M.:
Strategy, Models, and Imperatives

The primary team got together and was given hard copies of the following:

- The crisis response scenario
- All scenarios from the previous day, the associated cost, market, and operational models, and the impacts on the CEO's company (with probabilities)
- The challenges to each scenario

The primary team then updated the war room facilitators with the news. The CEO wanted to add an e-commerce strategy for the company to the war room agenda. The facilitators were not surprised, and quickly moved to incorporate the CEO's request. Chaos then broke out. It appeared that e-commerce meant everything from trading and fulfilling orders on-line to basic EDI transactions to the senior executives. The facilitators quickly took an unscheduled break and arranged for an expert to level-set the executives on the definition of e-commerce.

Exhibit 1-4. Business-to-business e-commerce forecast.

Worldwide Acceptance Grows beyond U.S.

Worldwide e-commerce to grow
from $170 billion in 1999 to over
$7.29 trillion in 2004; 7% of the
global economy

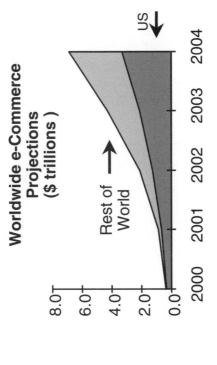

**Worldwide e-Commerce
Projections
($ trillions)**

Rest of
World

US

2000   2001   2002   2003   2004

0.0   2.0   4.0   6.0   8.0

Source: Dataquest, January 21, 2000.

Internet Commerce—Categories and Companies

Using state-of-the-art video-conferencing technology, the expert framed his definition of e-commerce. His presentation was titled *Internet Commerce Business Models.* In the overview, Internet commerce was divided into four main e-commerce role groups, as shown in Exhibit 1-5. The first group is the community, which includes a community provider. The community provider can be an affinity group and a customer community. Examples of affinity group companies are ICQ, Talkcity, Geocities, Tripod, and Motley Fool. Examples of customer community companies are America On-Line (AOL), PlasticPlatform, WebMD, PetroConnect, and Drums.

The second group is context, which includes the context provider. The context provider can be a general portal, a niche portal, referral agents, or a directory provider. Examples of general portal companies are Yahoo!, Lycos, Excite, AOL.com, MSN.com, InfoSeek.com, Bigfoot.com, and Netscape.com. Niche portal company examples are Women.com, Teen.com, Brides.com, CnetBuilder.com, Developer.com, and iVillage. Referral agent company examples are AutoByTel, Rent.net, Computers.com, Shop.com, Activebuyersguide, MySimon.com, and Chemdex. Directory provider company examples are yellow pages, business-to-business pages, chambers of commerce, business/industry associations, BigYellow, and MapQuest.

The third group is content, which includes the content provider. The content provider can be an information provider, a niche content provider, a bill aggregator, or a digital product provider. Information provider companies range from ESPN.com and CNN.com to Lexis-Nexis and WSJ (*The Wall Street Journal*) Interactive. Niche content provider companies include NBA.com, NHL.com, and specific associations like the American Automobile Association (AAA). Bill aggregator companies are represented by Citibank, Transpoint, and Checkfree. Digital product provider companies include Netscape, Microsoft, and Real Networks.

Exhibit 1-5. Internet commerce defined.

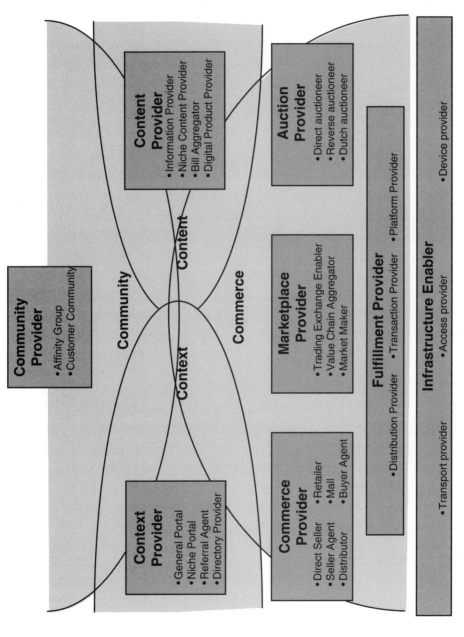

Community Provider
•Affinity Group
•Customer Community

Content Provider
•Information Provider
•Niche Content Provider
•Bill Aggregator
•Digital Product Provider

Auction Provider
•Direct auctioneer
•Reverse auctioneer
•Dutch auctioneer

Context Provider
•General Portal
•Niche Portal
•Referral Agent
•Directory Provider

Commerce Provider
•Direct Seller   •Retailer
•Seller Agent   •Mall
•Distributor   •Buyer Agent

Marketplace Provider
•Trading Exchange Enabler
•Value Chain Aggregator
•Market Maker

Community
Content
Context
Commerce

Fulfillment Provider
•Distribution Provider   •Transaction Provider   •Platform Provider

Infrastructure Enabler
•Transport provider   •Access provider   •Device provider

Source: Yobie Benjamin, Cap Gemini Ernst & Young, 1999, i2 PLANET99 Conference.

The fourth area is commerce, which includes commerce providers, marketplace providers, auction providers, fulfillment providers, and infrastructure enablers. Commerce providers include direct sellers like Dell and Gateway, seller agents like Chemdex.com, business-to-business distributors like Grainger.com, business-to-consumer retailers like Wal-Mart and Amazon.com, mall companies like mall.com and imall.com, and buyer agent companies like Priceline.com.

Marketplace providers include trading exchange enablers like E*Trade, Value Chain Aggregators like pcOrder and VerticalNet.com, and market makers like Digital Exchange and the New York Stock Exchange (NYSE). Auction providers include direct auctioneers like eBay, reverse auctioneers like Priceline.com, and Dutch auctioneers like Blomen Veiling Holland (BVH.NL). Fulfillment providers include distribution providers like SeaLand, United Parcel Service (UPS), and FedEx, transaction providers like Visa and AT&T, and platform providers like Cisco Systems. Infrastructure providers include transport providers like MCI WorldCom and IBM Global Network, access providers like all of the telecoms, and device providers like Cisco Systems, Nokia, and Compaq.

For each provider in each group, the expert provided the executive team with a high-level definition from which to work, as depicted in Exhibit 1-6. The expert described the definitions, value propositions, operational approaches, and profit mechanisms of each provider group. This detailed overview helped to demystify e-commerce for the executive group, and to associate names of companies with e-commerce roles.

After this crash course to level-set the definition of e-commerce, the primary group then broke into multifunctional groups to come up with strategies by (a) channel, (b) product line/brand, (c) geography (decided in advance by the executive sponsorship team), and (d) e-commerce, taking into account the various scenarios. Models were used to develop the new impacts and potential alliance partners within each e-commerce group. Members

Exhibit 1-6. Internet commerce role definitions.

Role Category	Definition
• Marketplace Provider	• Provides markets for exchanging goods and services between sellers and buyers over a network.
• Commerce Provider	• Markets, sells, and supports products and services over a network.
• Auction Provider	• Provides a platform for auction-based exchange of goods and services over a network.
• Context Provider	• Provides information and access to other sites.
• Community Provider	• Offers community services to groups of people.
• Content Provider	• Offers information services and support for digital products distribution over a network.
• Fulfillment Provider	• Supports fulfillment for executing transactions over a network.
• Infrastructure Provider	• Offers the infrastructure to support connectivity over a network.

Source: Yobie Benjamin, Cap Gemini Ernst & Young, 1999, i2 PLANET99 Conference.

crossed teams regularly, but a core team always remained. Part of this process was a "breaking the model" segment, during which specific people were assigned to teams to break the model, forcing each team to come up with contingency plans. The e-commerce group linked-up on-line with its e-strategy partners and accessed their respective databases. In addition, using on-line technology, the e-commerce group gathered information concerning what e-commerce strategies were currently being used by leading companies in similar manufacturing industries. These strategies were mapped into the high-level e-commerce roles map provided by the e-commerce expert that morning.

By mid-afternoon, the following was determined by the entire primary group:

- Crisis survival plan
- Reformulated strategic direction
- New and existing products
- New and existing markets
- New and existing channels
- Information systems initiatives
- Operational models and imperatives
- Any organizational issues
- Impacts on the company's finances (P&L, balance sheet, customers, market share, and shareholder value)
- High-level e-commerce strategic direction, including potential e-commerce provider partners

As always, this information was captured electronically on preset templates (and on some free-form space), and was displayed and printed out.

Dinner was served, and the teams worked through the evening to prepare a complete plan and model. The session officially closed at 8:00 P.M., but teams were able to carry on until they finished. The primary team was thankful that the CEO had to attend his daughter's sixteenth birthday party, and was unable to attend their working dinner.

Wednesday, 8:00 A.M.:
Execution

The primary team felt that they had just produced a few months' worth of work in little more than two days. They were very tired but were soon energized by the day's agenda. The day focused on execution, which was right in the strike zone for many of the primary team members.

The new models that had been developed on Tuesday were presented to the senior staff. Their comments and challenges were noted (remember that they were part of the development process on the previous two days). A two-page executive summary was e-mailed to the CEO. Concurrence was reached on the essential points with the CEO, who used the executive summary for his next conference call with an analyst. The CEO was happy with the progress . . . and the birthday party had gone well.

The primary group was then broken into smaller groups to develop detailed execution and communications plans (with accountabilities) based on all the work done thus far. This continued until mid-afternoon, when results were collated and presented. Each senior executive had the remainder of the afternoon to review the execution and communications plans with his or her direct reports and to make any final modifications. The deadline for final modifications was 8:00 P.M. so that the team would be prepared for the all-important exercise in the morning.

This part of the process was critical. Rapid consensus is an absolute necessity when responding to a crisis. The last thing anybody needed was to be in a "paralysis by analysis" environment. The key here was the deadline to drive the consensus and produce the final execution and communication plans.

Thursday, 9:00 A.M.: Debrief and Finalize

The facilitators and essential members of the primary team worked through the night collating the execution and communication plans from each senior executive. All operational models, financial models, and execution and communications plans were assembled into a draft of the CEO report. What was needed was the polishing of the executive summary, the learnings from the process, and areas to be reviewed in the future.

The war room team and the company's executive sponsors got together to debrief and prepare the final report for the CEO and board of directors. This combined group started by revisiting the CEO's original questions to ensure that each one had been addressed. These questions were:

- How could the CEO quickly stabilize his current operations and make the necessary decisions to invest globally and in e-commerce?
- How could the CEO ensure that his executive staff was aligned in the new company vision and supportive of the restructuring steps during this time of crisis?
- How could the CEO pull all of this together in a plan that would signal to Wall Street, his customers, and his employees that he was in control?
- How could the CEO be assured that all of his actions supported the primary drivers of shareholder value?

Satisfied that they had addressed the CEO's questions, the group prepared the final presentation for the CEO and board of directors. In addition, the executive team agreed to look at several areas in more depth using the war room for their scenario-planning. These areas included

- Outsourcing nonessential, non–core competency areas
- Supply chain and manufacturing strategy and design

- Boosting shareholder value strategy
- New product development and product lifecycle management strategy
- Information systems design and development
- Customer management strategy and design
- Merger and acquisition decisions, strategy, execution
- E-business strategy, including e-procurement, e-fulfillment, the use of trade exchanges, and potential e-commerce provider partners

The CEO and the board of directors welcomed the completeness of the crisis response plan. They especially appreciated its connectivity to P&L impact, necessary capital appropriations, and the inclusion of an e-commerce strategic direction. At the end of the board presentation, the CEO informed the senior staff that this was the beginning of a new era for their company. He instructed his senior staff to get another good night's rest because he expected their execution of the crisis response plan to be as fast as its development. The stunned senior staff looked at one another with amazement. However, they all were surprised by the speed at which they were able to respond. Many of them began talking with one another about how to accelerate execution as they left the boardroom. The CEO smiled as they left the room and thought that it was only the second time that he had smiled all week—the first had been for pictures during his daughter's birthday party.

THE CEO AND CRISIS RESPONSE—THE TEST OF TRUE LEADERSHIP

When a crisis occurs, the true test of leadership for a CEO and his or her company is the usual result. Strong CEOs respond quickly, decisively, and with a vision for opportunity. Weak CEOs frequently respond in a delayed, defensive, and confused manner. There is also no hiding when a crisis occurs. All eyes (of the consumers, shareholders, communities, and employees) and cameras are focused on the CEO and his or her response.

The use of a strong crisis response process and intelligent e-business technology (for example, a war room) helps the CEO be fact-based and forward-looking within a short period of time. Intelligence and speed, when integrated into a company's operations and strategic direction, can produce scenarios for CEOs so that they can respond to a crisis from a position of strength. This response can range from rapid stabilization of current operations to new investments in e-commerce and global operations to new product innovations. Whatever the CEO's choice, his or her chances improve significantly with help from procedures like the war room, which signals to Wall Street, customers, communities, and employees that he or she is in control and that shareholder value is protected as best as possible.

The most important question is: Why wait for a crisis to reinvent your company at Internet speed? Thanks to technology and intelligent e-business systems, the competitive landscape is changing at Internet speed. Winners and losers are being determined and recategorized daily. The market and time is waiting for no one. The time to act is now.

2

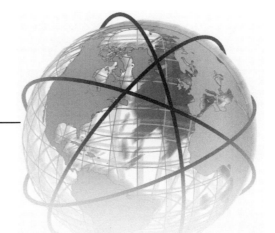

LET'S MAKE
A DEAL?

INTRODUCTION

It is 10:00 A.M. on a hot, muggy August morning on the East Coast, and the chief executive officer of a Fortune 500 manufacturing company that produces consumer products is headed with a sense of dread to a meeting with his board of directors. He knows that he will spend the next several hours fielding difficult questions to which he has few answers. Revenue and profits are down because the company is losing its market share to competitors. The CEO's greatest fear is that his job is in jeopardy. If he cannot quickly move the company in a new direction, the board will find someone else who can. His golden parachute provides plenty of financial security, but he is concerned about his legacy and does not want to suffer the embarrassment of being replaced.

When he had taken over the company ten years ago, the CEO had initiated a major reengineering project and had achieved significant cost savings. The board was very happy in those days when profitability climbed because of his cost-saving measures. In addition to a 10 percent reduction in the workforce, the CEO had also achieved savings in transportation and purchasing expenditures, reductions in inventory, and the closing of two distribution facilities. Because of these actions, the company's earnings steadily increased. The stock price responded in a positive way for many years. Recently, however, high-tech companies that were a fraction of his company's size were being rewarded with market capitalizations that far exceed the market cap of his company.

THE CONSOLIDATION HEADACHE

During the past year, the CEO's company experienced a volume decline that caused the stock price to stall. Although revenues were up slightly, they had hit a wall because of price increases and declining volumes. Future revenue growth was seriously in doubt. Contributing to the pricing pressures was rapid consolidation in the grocery industry. Companies like The Kroger Company and Fred Mayer, Safeway and Randalls/ Tom Thumb, and the Ahold acquisitions created large grocery retailers with significant purchasing leverage. Because his company had not launched any truly new and innovative products in the past few years, these megagrocers were demanding more pricing, promotion, and advertising concessions from his company.

As the CEO ponders how to address the board's concerns, he receives a telephone call from a security analyst that has followed his company for years. The analyst asks a quick question about his e-commerce strategy. The CEO doesn't have a quick answer, and promises to get back to him.

E-COMMERCE STRATEGY

Although the company was slow to enter the e-commerce arena, the CEO does not believe that its products are conducive to direct sale to consumers over the Internet. Some of his retail customers are offering the company's products through their Web sites, so the products are already available on-line. His executive committee has been telling him "not to worry about this Internet stuff because our consumers will never want to buy direct from us over the Internet." The committee has been recommending that the company allocate more funds to trade promotions. Its members believe that investment in an Internet capability would be a waste of time and money.

However, as the CEO sat in his den watching CNN and reading *The Wall Street Journal* one night, he realized there is much more to doing business over the Internet than offering products to his consumers. His company has never discussed Internet technologies in the business-to-business arena except for a few times when the purchasing director recommended changing the transmission of purchase orders to suppliers from EDI to transmission via the Web. Now that he thinks about it, the CEO notes that several security analysts had, in fact, made note of his company's lack of an Internet strategy. Perhaps the company was losing sales because of its inability to collaborate with its customers, suppliers, and employees over the Internet. His executives were so focused on the business-to-consumer side of e-commerce that they bypassed the whole business-to-business side. What made matters worse was that the business-to-business side of e-commerce actually pulls the network supply-chain partners closer together and closer to serving the end customer!

LACK OF CUSTOMER FOCUS

As he weaves his way through traffic, the CEO realizes that the fundamental problem is that the company has lost its customer focus. Although the company's number one and number two performance measures are on-time delivery and a complete order, the industry is changing its definition of customer intimacy. Lack of collaboration is only one example of poor relations with their customers. The CEO had been so intent on cost-cutting and efficiency that he and the company lost their connection to the customer—both the retail customer and the final consumer.

The sound of his beeper interrupts his thought process. He looks down and sees an urgent message coming across the screen. The message is from his chief operations officer informing him that their largest customer, TastyFoods, has just introduced a private-label product that competes with their number-one-selling product. This customer represents 20 percent of their total sales in this product. The CEO's blood pressure starts to rise as he realizes that this board meeting will be even worse than he had anticipated. How could this happen without having any advance warning? The thought of major customers concurrently becoming active competitors with private label products is unnerving. This is a loud and clear wake-up call. The challenge of being customer-focused suddenly became a lot more complicated!

The CEO's thoughts drift to a similar situation involving Procter & Gamble and Wal-Mart. In August 1999, Wal-Mart introduced a private-label laundry detergent called Sam's American Choice that competes head-on with Tide from P&G. Tide has approximately 38.6 percent of the laundry detergent market, and P&G is one of Wal-Mart's biggest suppliers. Sam's American Choice is also priced 25 to 30 percent lower than Tide, and is expected to be in all of Wal-Mart's stores. Wal-Mart accounts for approximately 20 percent of all laundry detergent sales in the United States.[1] Major retailers are becoming major customers and major competitors. The key for consumer-product manufacturers resides in outstanding brands that dominate categories and are priced more competitively than private-label products. Developing outstanding brands must involve customer connectivity and innovation. The battle is on for consumer recognition of just who is the brand—the consumer-product company or the retailer.

The CEO's beeper comes to life again as he asks himself what else could possibly go wrong today. This message is from a prominent member of the board indicating that its members would like to discuss his response to the TastyFoods situation at the meeting this afternoon. He realizes now that his only alternative in the boardroom is to ask for more time to address the situation. He has no answers but knows that he needs to get them quickly. He also knows that the board may give him a little slack due to his past record, but not much. The days of studying a problem for three months and then discussing it for another three months before reaching a decision are over. Quick action is required, and those businesses that are not agile enough to keep up are quickly gone. He will ask for one month to come up with a plan of attack.

The board meeting goes as well as could be expected. After the CEO cashes in on all his goodwill accumulated over the past ten years, the board agrees to give the CEO one month to develop a plan. Immediately upon returning to his office, the CEO calls an emergency meeting of his executive staff and briefs them on the urgency of the situation. He then begins asking them some tough questions. He realizes the plan cannot be one that each of his vice presidents can work on individually. The answer lies in tightly connecting sales, marketing, and the supply chain. These operating units' boundaries must become even more blurred to ensure a quick and successful implementation plan. Changing corporate performance measures and linking them to customer intimacy may be the first place to start.

The CEO sets the stage indicating that the purpose of this initial executive staff meeting will be to ensure that they all have a firm grasp of the issues. Then they will follow up in several days' time to plot solutions and strategies.

CUSTOMER MANAGEMENT OR ADMINISTRATIVE MANAGEMENT?

The first person on the hot seat is the TastyFoods account manager. She nervously explains that relations with this account have been a bit rocky lately. Discussions with Tasty-Foods often seemed to center around trade-deal terms and invoice and billing problems rather than on any discussion of consumer preferences. Deals had become so complex that billing problems were inevitable, and the account manager seemed to be spending most of her time trying to sort out invoice issues.

Relations with TastyFoods hit rock bottom last June. To make corporate sales goals for the second quarter, prices were reduced and customers "loaded" with product in late June. However, TastyFoods operates under a different deal structure and was not involved in that forward buying. The problem was that the company was out of stock by the end of June when a TastyFoods order was received. The order could not be completely filled for a week, and the TastyFoods shelves went out of stock for some key products. To make matters worse, TastyFoods was running a large advertising campaign on one of those items that week. The company had no forewarning of that advertising campaign, and was not able to react quickly. It may have been at that time that TastyFoods made the decision to develop a private-label brand and have a substitute option for future promotions.

Deal-loading, invoice problems, and customers becoming competitors are the serious events affecting the CEO's business. However, these events accentuated the symptoms of an even greater problem of how to drive profitable growth in a mature business.

PROFITABLE GROWTH

As all eyes are turned to the CEO, he relays the message that all of them, including himself, need to take responsibility for this situation and move forward in a positive constructive way. Their goal will be to improve their branding, develop a customer focus, and achieve growth—profitable growth. The emphasis here is on *profitable* growth, as illustrated in Exhibit 2-1. Profitable growth is one of the five drivers of shareholder value. Profitable growth involves growing revenues by focusing on products and customers, which maximizes profitability.

Although the CEO knows that his company's past problem has been its excessive focus on cost control with insufficient concern for the customer, he does not want to go overboard in the other direction and push toward higher revenues without concern for the bottom line. He is not interested in achieving sales at any cost. He wants to develop a plan whereby revenues will grow and his company, as well as his customers, will be profitable. They need to understand which of their customers and products are most profitable and then focus on increased

Exhibit 2-1. The five drivers of shareholder value.

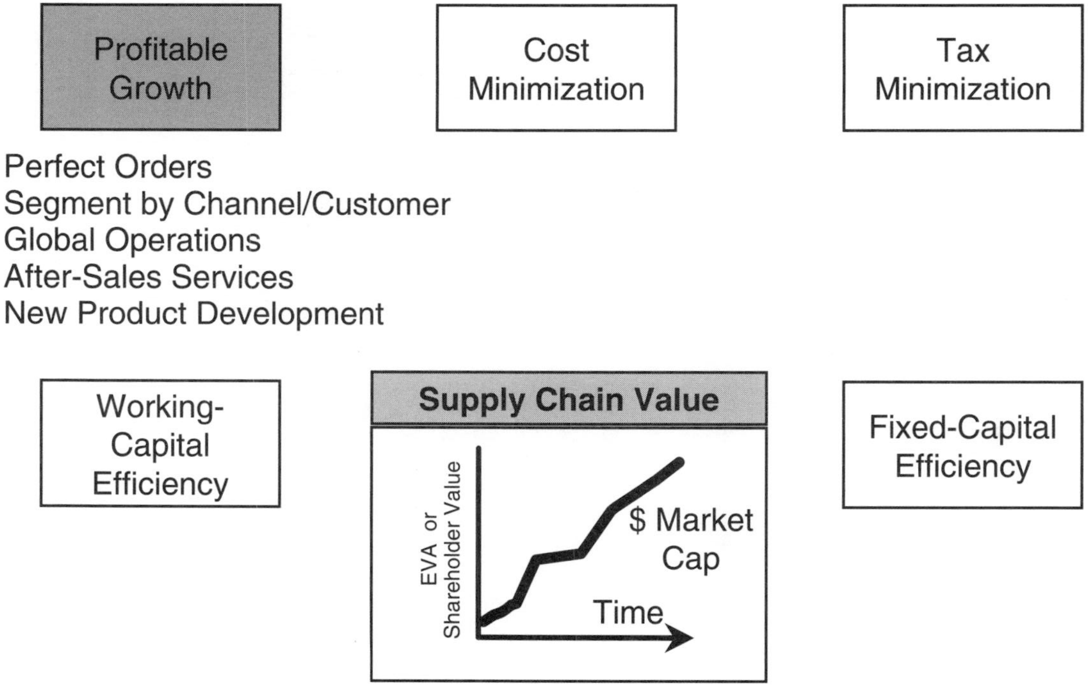
Profitable Growth
Cost Minimization
Tax Minimization
Perfect Orders
Segment by Channel/Customer
Global Operations
After-Sales Services
New Product Development
Working-Capital Efficiency
Supply Chain Value
EVA or Shareholder Value
$ Market Cap
Time
Fixed-Capital Efficiency

Source: Cap Gemini Ernst & Young.

volumes for those customers and products. Technology certainly would be one of the keys to future success.

SIMPLIFY COMPLEXITY; FOCUS ON VELOCITY

Consumer-products companies can have hundreds or thousands of line items. Frequently, these companies have the 80/20 or 85/15 rule, with 80 to 85 percent of their sales resulting from 15 to 20 percent of their line items.

The CEO was concerned about his sales-to-line-item mix. He wondered whether his consumers were truly interested in his 1,000+ line items. In many cases, line-item proliferation only serves to confuse the consumer (not to mention the operations staff of the manufacturer). By simplifying the product portfolio, consumer-products companies provide their consumers with clearer choices. They can also build greater brand equity with stronger brand recognition and focused trade spending.

The average grocery store in the United States today carries about 31,000 SKUs (stock-keeping units), 20 to 50 percent more than they carried in 1993. Yet consumers have less time to shop and are confused by the wide array of product options available to them. Twenty-two percent of products sell at a rate of less than one item per month per store.[2] Our CEO feared that many of his line items fit into this latter category. He jotted down a note to initiate an SKU rationalization program.

To compound this problem, 80 percent of the CEO's business comes from the twenty-five largest retail customers. At the current rate of mergers and acquisitions, this percentage would grow still larger in the coming years. The remaining business is divided up among thousands of other customers. The question then is what type of service is provided to each customer and what is the cost to serve. Unfortunately, it appears that all of their customers are treated equally. There is no differentiation of service across customers. The smallest corner grocery store receives a similar level of service as TastyFoods, the largest food chain in the country. So, while last June thousands of small stores were overstocked with their product due to the latest promotional push, the shelves of TastyFoods were empty. Obviously, this situation needs to change. Although no one suggests that they drop the small customers, there needs to be a change in how their large customers are being treated and a better understanding of customer profitability. Clearly, since the majority of their business comes from a small number of customers, they need to be tightly linked with these customers. Customer segmentation was also noted for a future program with the executives.

They turn now to the marketing and accounting departments for a discussion of customer profitability. Unfortunately, the problem they confront is lack of data to determine which customers are profitable and which are not. The company has so many different types of promotion and pricing schemes that it is nearly impossible to determine profitability. Even more difficult to understand is which promotions are profitable and which are not. The advertising and marketing budget is 10 percent of sales, and two-thirds of that is being spent on trade promotions. No one, however, can provide data on the benefit or return that the company is receiving from that investment.

PROMOTIONS AND THE SUPPLY CHAIN

Because of the current crisis, it becomes apparent that the cost of promotions is not just direct marketing dollars. There is a tremendous operational expense involved with the supply chain volatility caused by promotional activity. In addition to the customer service issues they had just experienced, the irregular demand patterns caused by the promotions result in disruptions and excess costs in manufacturing, warehousing, transportation, and inventory costs. Because of the irregularity of the sales patterns, demand on manufacturing is irregular, requiring significant overtime at some points during the year and very low capacity utilization at others. The same is true for warehousing and transportation; the product flow has significant peaks and valleys that disrupt operations. In order to manage this sporadic demand and still meet customer needs, significant levels of inventory are maintained that, of course, add to the company's working capital requirements.

The practice of loading has caused their current problems. This practice is common throughout the retail and consumer products industries. It is the result of a company's efforts to meet its financial objectives and the sales and profit expectations of the security analysts. Failure to meet financial goals can have a detrimental impact on share price. Therefore, as the end of each quarter approaches, if it appears that the company will not meet its financial goals, financial incentives are offered to customers to accept more product than they would normally purchase. Therefore, the retailers are forward-buying, and building inventories with significant price incentives to do so. Of course, sales at the start of the next quarter will be lower, because the retailer is using up existing inventories. Therefore, as the close to the next quarter approaches, loading is again required to meet or beat the previous quarter's sales. It then becomes a never-ending cycle, with loading a way of life with all of its inherent inefficiencies and costs.

Given all the disruptions that the promotions cause, the question remains as to what benefit is being derived. What is the positive impact on sales? A trade promotion program is only successful if it results in increased purchases by the consumer and, therefore, increased revenues for the company. The CEO suspects that the majority of the promotional impact was either from sales cannibalized from other products or from forward-buying by the consumer. In either of these cases, the net benefit of the current promotional activity is in serious question. It was only in cases that the promotion actually increased consumer consumption or cannibalized from other brands that they would benefit. Unfortunately, they had no data to assess the true impact.

Even worse, it seems that the focus on promotional discounts and activity takes the focus away from the consumer. The marketing vice president admits that, unfortunately, much of the time his salespeople spend with accounts is centered on discussions about allowances, rebates, stocking fees, and retail assistance rather than on discussions as to what the consumer is interested in buying.

ECR AND GOOD INTENTIONS

Efficient Consumer Response (ECR) is an initiative the company has been involved with since 1992 in the grocery supply chain. The objective was to coordinate activities across enterprises in the supply chain, thus reducing costs in the system and improving customer service. It was initially estimated that these initiatives would reduce inventory in the system by 41 percent to provide savings of $30 billion and that dry grocery lead times would be reduced from 104 days of supply to 61.

Unfortunately, seven years after the initial study, results are not as significant as had been hoped for. It is interesting that many of the problems plaguing this company are also inhibiting the success of ECR initiatives. These problems include continued forward-buying, ineffective communications between retailers and manufacturers with respect to promotional activity, and lack of information technology that would allow real-time information sharing.[3] The CEO realizes that his company will need to solve its own problems instead of waiting for an industry initiative to solve the company's problems. He decides to focus on what the leading companies in his industry are doing.

What's Next?

The week passes quickly, and the group reconvenes to plot strategy. The group first turns its attention to some of the leading practices adapted by companies that are achieving some success in realizing benefits. The following areas are selected for review:

- Category management with continuous replenishment
- Web-based item catalogs and data synchronization
- Scan-based trading
- Interfirm communications and coordination
- Performance monitoring
- Electronic transmittal of orders, demand, and shipment tracking information
- Everyday low price in place of promotional pricing
- Simplified pricing and standardized payment terms
- People functionally focused with a high percentage of their performance appraisal based on servicing sales and customer satisfaction
- Collaborative planning and forecasting

Now they need to focus on some essential initiatives. During the week, the TastyFoods account manager spent time with his account doing damage control but also developing plans on how the companies can work in closer collaboration. He found that TastyFoods has some very innovative ideas and is very interested in closer collaboration between the two companies. TastyFoods is very aware of the issues and problems that occur when it does not communicate and collaborate well with its suppliers. The problems that have marred its relationship with the CEO's company are the same issues that it is confronting with all of its suppliers. TastyFoods has been exploring ways in which it can work more collaboratively with its supplier and feels that close collaboration and information-sharing will result in a win-win situation for all involved. One area that Tasty-Foods requested to be reviewed was invoice deductions.

INVOICE DEDUCTIONS AND THE viaLink SOLUTION

The retail and consumer-products industries have been slow to adopt technology as compared to other industries. One area that represents a significant problem to the industry is the manual way that deals are made and handled. Historically, deals have included paper price-books that have housed item and price schedules. These paper price-books have resulted in manual tracking of every item by price and product. Purchase orders are frequently issued with the wrong pricing and item numbers. Therefore, deliveries are made to retailers with merchandise that references a purchase order with erroneous pricing and sometimes item information.

This sounds ominous, but the process is just getting started. Invoices issued by wholesaler-distributors or consumer-products manufacturers frequently do not match the paper price-book data on deal pricing. Therefore, there exists an army of people up and down the supply chain who deal with invoice reconciliations. It is estimated that invoice deductions represent a $40 billion problem for the industries.[4]

There is a Web-based start-up, called viaLink, that has created an on-line solution to this problem. ViaLink has created a Web-based catalog (syncLink) that allows item, price, and promotion information to electronically become data of record. This collaboration creates a common database for all deal-trading partners to access. It enables the synchronization of the deal data, thus aligning the purchase order, shipping order, invoice, and payables under one common data set. The result? The elimination of invoice deductions, as illustrated in Exhibit 2-2.

Exhibit 2-2. viaLink solution.

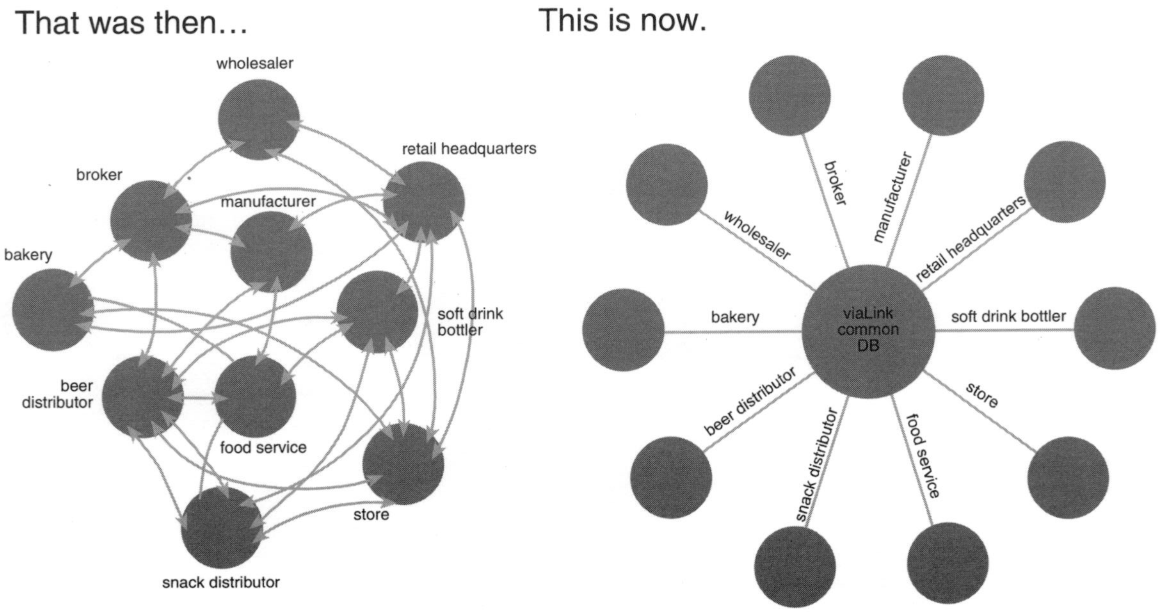

That was then...

This is now.

Source: viaLink.

SCAN-BASED TRADING

There is another type of technology-driven transformation occurring in the industry called scan-based trading (SBT). The viaLink solution actually enables the effective implementation of scan-based trading, as explained in Exhibit 2-3.

The first step in scan-based trading is the synchronization of the items, prices, and promotion allowances with the trading partners as the viaLink solution addresses. The next two steps are to share critical point-of-sale (POS) data between trading partners and to establish a new networked supply-chain process that streamlines how consumer-products companies and wholesaler-distributors do business with retailers.

The sharing of the critical point-of-sale (POS) data between trading partners is not new in the industry. Many retailers have "sold" their POS data to augment anemic profit margins. Wal-Mart took this sharing to a new level when they started to share POS data to enable suppliers to produce needed quantities of products for their stores. Slowly, other retailers are starting to look at sharing POS data with their suppliers to drive supply chain process improvements.

The Web-based item catalog and data synchronization breakthroughs by viaLink and the initial data sharing of POS data between retailers have combined to allow for serious testing of scan-based trading in the industry. (The GMA SBT pilot results are scheduled to be released at press time.) This involves the direct store delivery (DSD) of merchandise to stores with the items, pricing, and trading allowances stored in a common database. The suppliers deliver receive the merchandise and place it on the shelves. As the merchandise is sold and the items scanned at the grocery store, an electronic payable is immediately set up by the retailer. This payable accesses the pricing and trade allowance information from the common database, and a check is issued or payment is made electronically.

Exhibit 2-3. Three steps to viaLink scan-based technology.

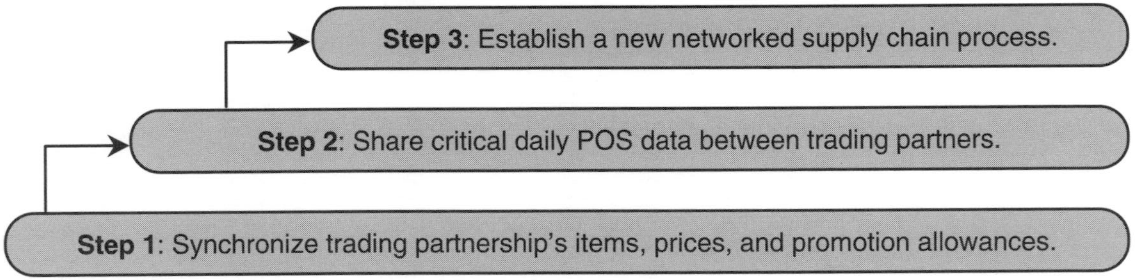

Step 1: Synchronize trading partnership's items, prices, and promotion allowances.

Step 2: Share critical daily POS data between trading partners.

Step 3: Establish a new networked supply chain process.

Source: viaLink.

Scan-based trading is now being rolled out by selected retailers with their direct store delivery partners. The question for DSD suppliers and brokers is not "if," but "when and how fast" they implement SBT.

The real power of these technological advances is the Web-based data and information synchronization between trading partners from initial deal to purchase over the scanner to final cash settlement. The inclusion of a Web-based catalog, data synchronization, and scan-based trading into his emerging e-commerce strategy excites the CEO. (Data synchronization is mandatory for SBT.) What was missing were the collaborative process and the technology to pull it all together.

CPFAR and TradeMatrix™

In the consumer-products industry, there have been many efforts to institute collaborative relationships between manufacturers and retailers. The most recent attempts have centered on collaborative planning, forecasting, and replenishment (CPFAR), as illustrated in Exhibit 2-4. There have been a few instances of one-to-one collaboration using CPFAR, but widespread implementation and success in this arena have eluded the industry. One of the problems with CPFAR is not with its concept, but with the fact that it represents a one-to-one collaborative *partner* relationship between trading partners. This relationship is contrary to the "Let's make a deal" philosophy that has permeated the industry for decades.

Although TastyFoods must coordinate with many suppliers, CPFAR requires them to set up the relationships one at a time. TastyFoods is now looking at a new approach, a TradeMatrix, that allows the corporation to collaborate with many of its suppliers in one environment. Its goal is to dramatically improve communication and collaboration with all of its suppliers. In this environment, real-time collaboration and information-sharing eliminates many communications issues that

Exhibit 2-4. Collaborative planning, forecasting, and replenishment.

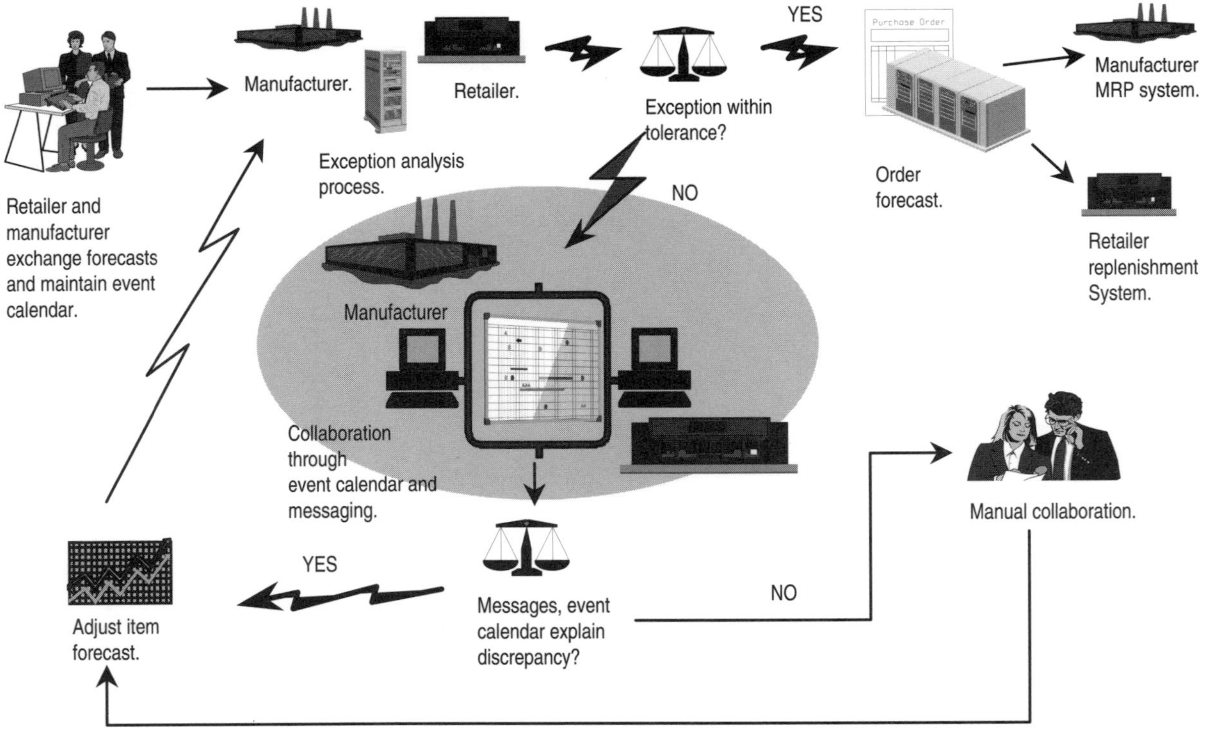

Retailer and manufacturer exchange forecasts and maintain event calendar.
Manufacturer.
Retailer.
Exception analysis process.
Exception within tolerance?
YES
NO
Purchase Order
Order forecast.
Manufacturer MRP system.
Retailer replenishment System.
Manufacturer
Collaboration through event calendar and messaging.
Messages, event calendar explain discrepancy?
YES
NO
Adjust item forecast.
Manual collaboration.

Source: Collaborative Planning Forecasting and Replenishment Committee of the Uniform Code Council, and Cap Gemini Ernst & Young.

have plagued TastyFoods' relationship with its suppliers. TastyFoods will be an anchor retailer with TradeMatrix and will recommend that its suppliers also join. A six-step process defines the collaborative process with each supplier.

1. The supplier generates a statistical forecast and new product introduction information and sends it to Tasty-Foods.

2. TastyFoods reviews the demand forecast and exceptions. At this point, TastyFoods can view new product information as well as see demand-and-supply mismatches where the supplier may not be able to meet forecasted demand.

3. TastyFoods modifies or updates the forecasts and sends them back to the supplier. At this point TastyFoods indicates, for example, where it anticipates increased demand due to promotions it will be running.

4. The seller sends back the supply-plan information and offers alternatives for exceptions. The seller has completed the demand/supply matching process and is able to report what it is able to produce and deliver.

5. TastyFoods reviews the supply-plan information and looks for exceptions.

6. TastyFoods sends back updated demand information. If there are items that cannot be supplied, TastyFoods has the option to update the demand information and order substitute products.

TastyFoods is hoping to have all of its major suppliers join the TradeMatrix. In this way it can easily coordinate its demand and promotional schedule with each of its suppliers and thus be assured of inventory when it is required. If they had been operating the TradeMatrix last June, all of the issues that have marred their relationship probably would not have occurred.

The group reflects upon the technology-driven solutions presented. They believe that they will develop the following capabilities by implementing identified solutions:

- *Catalog-Item Maintenance.* Allows them to dynamically create and update their product offerings. Allows retailers to immediately see the latest product introductions.
- *Price Synchronization.* Synchronizes item-pricing, promotion, and price authorization information between manufacturers and retailers within a specific channel.
- *Sales Forecasting.* Enables collaboration between the merchandise plan of the retailers and the sales plan of the manufacturer based on the CPFAR model.
- *Order Forecasting.* Allows manufacturers and retailers to reach consensus on near-term order forecasts.
- *Replenishment.* Continuous replenishment capability based on day-to-day retail-store demand.

THE FUTURE

Later in the day, the CEO sits back and mentally reviews the results of the meeting and the new direction they have set. The meeting has set his thoughts in motion with respect to the direction of the industry. He lets his mind wander to ponder further innovations that could occur in the coming years. Clearly, the key is linking electronically to their customers. There is so much consolidation occurring in the retail industry that a very small number of customers will continue to represent a very high percentage of their overall sales in the future. The link to those customers needs to be tight, and the degree of customization that his company can provide to customers will be significant due to their small numbers. Many future possibilities race across his mind.

With the help of selected industry experts, the CEO assembles three different scenarios representing how the retail and consumer-products industries may evolve.

SCENARIO 1: ANNUAL CONTRACTS VERSUS "BUYING ON DEAL"

One way to quickly connect to customers and link the supply chain from supplier to store shelf is through changing the way consumer products are bought and sold. As stated earlier, the majority of the industry still buys "on-deal." This method, often called deal-loading, involves the grocer or distributor purchasing large quantities of product immediately before the manufacturer's promotion ends. Because the discount is given on quantity ordered during a specified period, buyers purchase enough to carry them over to the next manufacturer's promotion. Frequently, this method also involves the disposition of excess inventory, often called diverting. Deal-loading creates a significant amount of cost because of demand and production fluctuations resulting in plant overtime, premium transportation on raw materials, and excess finished goods inventory.

Another action that causes an imbalance in the even flow of goods from manufacturer and consumer is the use of bracket pricing. Because of the large amount of product proliferation, it is difficult for a grocer to sell a full truckload of a manufacturer's product on a weekly basis. However, the grocer is given incentives from the manufacturer to purchase a mix of product in full pallet/full truckload quantities. This causes an uneven flow of goods though the supply chain. This, coupled with the account manager's need to "make his or her number" every month, is another reason why the volume of product flowing from the manufacturer to the grocer is so dramatically unstable compared to the consumer's demand out the front door of the grocery store. Manufacturers spend too much time and energy on smaller distribution savings while tripping over dollars that could have been realized through annual pricing models and continuous product-flow supply chains.

These annual contracts help support stronger supply chain operations. Annual contracts can be warehoused in a data warehouse and used to forecast demand. Of course, promotions, new products, and competitive responses in the marketplace must be accounted for in the forecast. In fact, the annual contracts should detail what, when, and how promotions take place. Good contracts will even offer incentives to both parties on the performance of the brand so that the grocer and the manufacturer have joint rather than competing goals throughout the year. With the consolidation in the retail industry producing a few very large retailers, the next step in networked supply chain effectiveness will be the movement of these megaretailers toward annual contracts with their suppliers.

SCENARIO 2: ALLOCATING AND "SELLING" OF PRODUCTION CAPACITY TO RETAIL CUSTOMERS

Scenario number two encompasses large retail customers having real-time input and *ownership* of the product mix scheduled for production by suppliers. Customers would, in essence, reserve or "buy" a percentage of the manufacturing capacity of its suppliers within defined parameters. They would specify packaging, price points, features, etc. Product would primarily be made to customer specification, thus eliminating current problems caused by an excessive number of SKUs, obsolete inventory, and demand/supply matching issues. Customers would have a direct portal into a company's ordering and production systems and real-time information about order status. Because the retailer would be setting the price points and promotion structures, and ordering according to those decisions, all the waste and confusion in the current system would be eliminated, and a truly synchronized networked supply chain would emerge. Of course, reserved production capacity has a price, whether it is used or not. The use of a trading exchange within the networked supply chain would provide an outlet for unused production capacity within defined trading partners.

SCENARIO 3: MANUFACTURERS MANAGING CATEGORIES *AND* GUARANTEEING SHELF-SPACE PROFITABILITY

The third scenario piques the CEO's interest. He wonders why retailers would want to bother owning production capacity and scheduling his company's production. The large retailers might want to choose one dominant manufacturer in each category and give that company responsibility for managing the category and related shelf space. The retailer would provide profitability guidelines and require the manufacturer to carry a certain percentage of competing brands, but otherwise would give them freedom to manage the category. Category management has been around for at least fifteen years. However, what is unique in this scenario is that the category manager guarantees a return to the retailer for each square foot and cubic foot of space managed. Beyond the guarantee, the returns per square foot and cubic foot of space managed would be split 50–50 with the retailer. The concept of guaranteed profitability for the retailer, with a greater risk/reward situation for the consumer-products manufacturer, is intriguing to the CEO. The CEO thinks that he really needs to be on top of his game to assume the risk associated with this scenario. However, it is one way to profitably grow the company if addressed in the proper manner.

PROFITABLE GROWTH— HOW TO GET STARTED

After reading about the issues confronting our hypothetical CEO in the consumer packaged goods industry, the questions in your mind, as an executive in this industry, are "What do I do now?" and "How do I get started?" We talk throughout the book about the five drivers of shareholder value: profitable growth, cost minimization, tax minimization, fixed-capital efficiency, and working-capital efficiency. In this industry, the essential focus needs to be on *profitable growth*. Of course, the other drivers continue to be important, but reengineering efforts in your company have probably already addressed many of the issues around cost minimization and working- and fixed-capital efficiencies. The key now is to drive profitable growth. The following is an eight-step process designed to help the executive to get started:

Profitable Growth

Step 1: Understand your customers' needs.

Step 2: Simplify your product line.

Step 3: Focus on your largest, most profitable customers.

Step 4: Link performance measure to customer satisfaction/loyalty.

Step 5: Develop strong brands.

Step 6: Simplify pricing and deal structures.

Step 7: Use Internet technology to collaborate with your customers.

Step 8: Become a leader in breakthrough e-commerce solutions.

Step 1: Understand your customers' needs. You need to work closely with both your retail customers and your consumers to understand their requirements. It is equally important that you understand consumer preferences beyond their requirements. Point of sale data, shelf-space category management tools, and overall market research will allow you to determine what products consumers really want—or do not want.

Step 2: Simplify your product line. Once customer and consumer requirements and needs are assessed, the executive team must take a closer look at their product portfolio. It is likely that it contains a significant number of products that are contributing minimally to revenue growth but are contributing little or nothing to your company's profitability. The additional products may create some growth, but not profitable growth. Why are you making all of these products? Your vice president of marketing may tell you that all of the products are needed to meet consumer needs and to have a well-rounded product line. However, the real reason may be that the marketing department has no incentive to reduce the product line. Your product managers are encouraged to develop new products each year, but there is little incentive to discontinue products, so the product line continues to grow. Marketing looks at the incremental sales from each product, without regard for the high investment in inventory and operating expense necessary to support the products. Not only are there millions of dollars tied up in inventory, but the cost of warehousing and maintaining these products in the line is enormous. Significantly streamlining the product line will not only reduce costs but will shift sales into products that are more profitable and reduce consumer confusion.

Step 3: Focus on your largest, most profitable customers. Because of the current rate of mergers and acquisitions, the number of retailers continues to shrink, and the emerging megaretailers are controlling larger percentages of the overall consumer market. You probably have a small number of customers that make up a high percentage of your sales. Many consumer-products executives believe that Wal-Mart represents 15 to 20 percent of a consumer-products company's business, with the next four major retailers making up 30 to 35 percent of their business. If these numbers are accurate, then a consumer-products company has approximately 50 percent of its business concentrated in five large accounts. Several consumer-products companies have major account focus teams to ensure that proper attention is given to these major customers. Keep those customers happy, because they are the keys to the profitable growth of your company.

Another factor is not to treat all customers the same. Your large customers demand high levels of service and responsiveness. Ensure that your organization, processes, and systems are set up to ensure that high level of service.

Step 4: Link performance measures to customer satisfaction/loyalty. To ensure that the primary goal of your company is keeping customers happy, tie the performance of your people to measures of customer satisfaction. For example, track perfect order rates of your large customers and then reward your people when high percentages are reached. Another measure would be major account team reviews by the customer. Factors such as sales, stock-outs, promotion effectiveness, issue resolution, invoice discrepancies and deductions, and ease of doing business are examples of areas for customer review. In addition, all employees within the company regardless of function should have some at-risk compensation tied to customer satisfaction.

Step 5: Develop strong brands. The profit margin for retailers on generic brands is significantly higher than on branded products. Therefore, they have large incentives to develop and sell generic products. In order for you, the consumer-products manufacturer, to maintain your shelf space and market share, you must create strong branding with your products. A weak brand is an invitation for the development of generic products with the resultant erosion of market share. Retailers are in the business to sell products. One way to have the retailers come to you is to have products that are in demand by consumers. Examples of strong branded products are Doritos, Campbell's soups, Tide, Heinz ketchup, and Coca-Cola.

Step 6: Simplify pricing and deal structures. In the management of your supply chain, you are one of the culprits in creating the variability that hinders your ability to operate smoothly and efficiently and provide the levels of customer service required to satisfy your customers and achieve profitable growth. If you tracked actual consumption of most consumer packaged-goods items, you would find it generally very stable and predictable. Yet, the demand patterns that a consumer packaged-goods company contends with are highly variable. The deal and promotional programs that you create contribute, in part, to this undesirable variability. To handle these erratic patterns, production must vary and high inventory levels be maintained or customer service suffers. None of these is an attractive alternative. However, some of this variability is in your control. Look at your pricing and deal structures, and simplify to encourage ordering patterns in line with actual consumer demand. Another way is to adopt Scenario 1, buying on annual contracts instead of buying on deal.

Step 7: Use Internet technology to collaborate with your customers. To create a true picture of consumer demand so that you can be responsive to your customers, you must work in collaboration with your large customers. You must understand their promotional programs and the actual point-of-sale consumer demand. To achieve this level of collaboration requires the technology of and participation in a trade exchange, such as TradeMatrix. Get involved, because this is the future. Those manufacturers who are not working in collaboration with their large customers and meeting high levels of customer service will soon find that they will be replaced.

Step 8: Become a leader in breakthrough e-commerce solutions. A critical success factor for profitable growth is to understand your customers' needs and respond to them quickly and efficiently. The Internet provides exciting, innovative technologies that allow you to link with your customers. Take advantage of them. For example, consider scan-based trading enabled by viaLink. Work with your customers to establish a new networked supply chain process that streamlines how consumer-products companies and wholesaler-distributors do business with retailers.

Summary

Although the above scenarios currently may be materializing in some form, we believe that technology and the hypercompetitiveness of the industry will drive significant change in the future. Web-based solutions like viaLink, scan-based trading, trading exchanges like TradeMatrix, and closer collaboration with trading partners for demand forecasting and supply planning (CPFAR) will contribute to an environment of change. Annual contracting will make some inroads into the time-tested, time-hardened, and inefficient practice of deal-loading. The large retailers will use their new size to reserve production capacity from suppliers for some of their key branded items.

The large retailers will also push for guaranteed returns on their shelf space from suppliers wishing to manage categories of products. The only things in question are how much, how far, and how fast.

The eight-step process will help the consumer-product executive to get started in a fact-based way. It all starts with the customer. Wins and losses are registered every time a product goes across a retailer's scanner. The battle is for control of the customer's wallet, or, in this industry, the customer's stomach!

Our CEO? He had his board meeting, and was given thirty days to present a new e-commerce strategy to the security analysts. It took thirty years to build his company, and the security analysts want to know how he will transform the company in thirty days. At least his team came up with a number of technology-enabling solutions to empower his networked supply chain and proceed with a plan. Time appears to wait for no one in the Internet economy!

NOTES

1. Emily Nelson, "For Wal-Mart, a Soap War Looms Against Mighty P&G," *The Wall Street Journal*, August 6, 1999, p. B1.
2. Ralph W. Drayer, "Procter & Gamble's Streamlined Logistics Initiatives," *Supply Chain Management Review*, Summer 1999, vol. 3, issue 2.
3. Judith Schmitz Whipple, Robert Frankel, and Kenneth Anselmi, "The Effect of Governance Structure on Performance: A Case Study of Efficient Consumer Response," *Journal of Business Logistics*, 1999, vol. 20, no. 2.
4. Discussions with Robert Noe during the F.M.I. Marketechniques Conference in San Francisco, February 2000.

3

SUPPLY CHAIN

INNOVATION

INTRODUCTION

The sun is just now coming up on the East Coast of the United States. It is early afternoon in Europe, and late at night in Asia. On the West Coast, there is still the peacefulness of the early morning predawn hours. The only sounds are from the wildlife and the investment bankers who keep Wall Street hours. Despite technology and after-hours trading, the world still seems to revolve around Wall Street hours.

In an exclusive neighborhood in Silicon Valley, there is a light on in the home office of the CEO of a major high-tech hardware manufacturer. Despite the peacefulness of the early morning hours, the CEO is experiencing a high level of anxiety and angst. The high-tech market is flying at Internet speed, with some still gaining altitude while others are dropping from the sky. His company is only moving at land-speed limits, not crashing, but not flying with the best.

The global personal computer (PC) market is the largest segment of the computer hardware industry. According to International Data Corp. (IDC), 113 million personal computers were shipped worldwide in 1999, and were worth $190 billion. Desktop units represented 80 percent, notebooks 17 percent, and PC servers 3 percent of this market segment. This market grew at 20+ percent from 1991 to 1995. From 1995 through 1998, this market segment drifted downward to a 15 percent growth rate. In 1999, the growth rate accelerated back to approximately 20 percent.[1]

The number of households "wired" for Internet access continues to expand. According to ZDNet's market research outfit Infobeads, the percentage of homes in the United States with personal computers grew from 38.5 percent in 1995 to 52.7 percent in mid-1999.[2] Experts at Cap Gemini Ernst & Young's high-tech practice estimate that this number will approach 70 percent by the year 2003. This household penetration expands the PC market in two ways. First, the number of households wired expands the number of PCs to be sold. Second, the more the households are wired for using the Internet, the more people will use the Internet, and the more people will be dependent on their PCs.

The personal computer contains only a few essential components. The central processing unit (CPU), the operating system, and the memory make up the heart of a PC. The CPU is usually manufactured by Intel or Advanced Micro Devices. Microsoft usually provides the operating system. (In fact, the dominance of Intel and Microsoft has given rise to the term "WinTel" in the industry.) Multiple suppliers provide the memory devices. Despite the limited number of essential components and suppliers, the configuration of the PC can be complex.

The consolidation in the PC industry has been accelerating. The top-five PC assemblers (Compaq, Dell, IBM, HP, and Gateway) controlled approximately 42 percent of the market in 1999.[3] Most experts believe that consolidation will continue to accelerate during the next five years.

WHAT IS DRIVING CHANGE IN THE PC INDUSTRY?

The reality is that many PC manufacturers provided direct innovation in the product itself for many years. However, because of the explosion of technological advances in PC components, this is no longer the case. The suppliers are now providing the direct innovation, with the PC manufacturers providing indirect innovation.

These technological changes from the component suppliers occur so quickly that PC-product life cycles average from three months to, at most, two years. It is estimated that 50 percent of the profits from PC products are achieved within the first three to six months of the life cycle.[4]

Another factor fueling the hypercompetitiveness is the deep discounting by suppliers when a new generation of processors, operating systems, or memory is introduced. These new generations of components are instantly in high demand. They also render the older generations of components to a much lower level of demand virtually overnight. Thus, you have an industry that demands instant response to the market on a day-to-day basis.

A demand is also created within each PC company for flexible, effective supply chain management that operates at Internet speed. There is no room for anything other than execution with speed. The stakes are too high. One market-share point is now worth $2 billion! Obsolescence can kill profit margins, yet loss of customers can kill a company.

FROM LINEAR SUPPLY CHAINS TO NETWORKED SUPPLY CHAINS

In the personal computer industry, the result of forces driving change in the industry is that supply chains are no longer linear. Before the technology explosion of the last five to seven years, supply chains moved product and information from suppliers to manufacturers to wholesalers/retailers in defined steps. Today, information moves independently of the product flows and at Internet speeds. The old supply chains have evolved into networked supply chains that rapidly network optimal partners with the right components, technology, and services for customers, as illustrated in Exhibit 3-1. These networked supply chains are extremely dynamic, allowing for companies to be included or excluded based upon technological advances, product life cycles, and customer preferences.

As illustrated in Exhibit 3-2, the networked supply chain solution manages the complexity of this dynamic network by

(text continues on page 62)

Exhibit 3-1. From linear supply chains to networked supply chains.

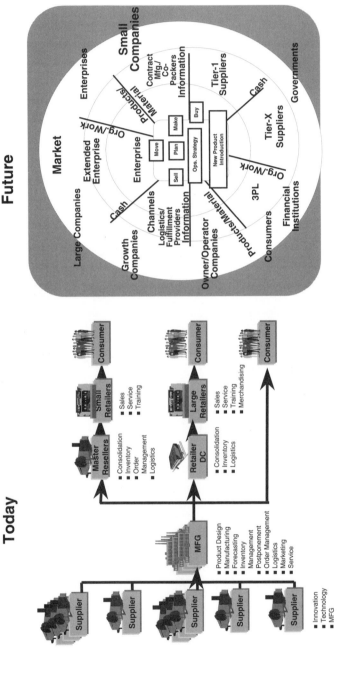

Source: Cap Gemini Ernst & Young.

Exhibit 3-2. Networked supply chain solutions.

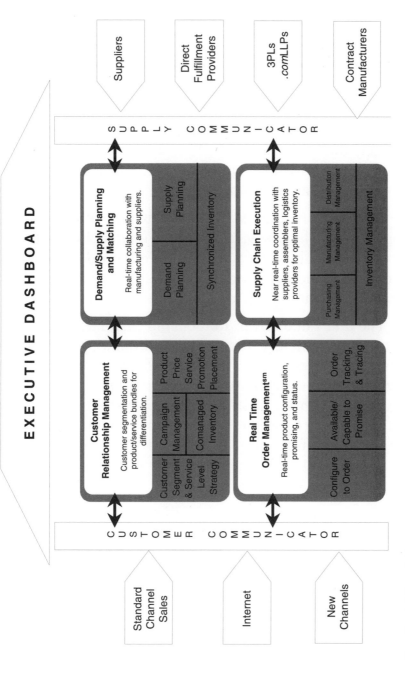

EXECUTIVE DASHBOARD

Suppliers

Direct Fulfillment Providers

3PLs
.comLLPs

Contract Manufacturers

SUPPLY COMMUNICATOR

Demand/Supply Planning and Matching

Real-time collaboration with manufacturing and suppliers.

Demand Planning

Supply Planning

Synchronized Inventory

Supply Chain Execution

Near real-time coordination with suppliers, assemblers, logistics providers for optimal inventory.

Purchasing Management

Manufacturing Management

Distribution Management

Inventory Management

Customer Relationship Management

Customer segmentation and product/service bundles for differentiation.

Customer Segment & Service Level Strategy

Campaign Management

Comanaged Inventory

Product
Price
Service
Promotion
Placement

Real Time Order Managementsm

Real-time product configuration, promising, and status.

Configure to Order

Available/ Capable to Promise

Order Tracking, & Tracing

CUSTOMER COMMUNICATOR

Standard Channel Sales

Internet

New Channels

Source: Cap Gemini Ernst & Young.

integrating sales and marketing activities with operational decision-making while synchronizing multiple supply chain partners. The supply side includes suppliers, direct fulfillment providers, logistics service providers or third-party logistics providers, and contract manufacturers. The supply side is linked to the value web through a supply communicator.

The demand side of the networked supply chain includes the standard channel sales (including customer direct) of the Internet, and new channels like kiosks at university bookstores. The supply side is linked to the networked supply chain through the customer communicator.

There are two essential value drivers in the networked supply chain. The first value driver is influencing customer demand based on inventory visibility. The second value driver is coordinating the networked supply chain with customer fulfillment expectations.

The first value driver, influencing customer demand based on inventory visibility, focuses on coordinating customer relationship management activities with demand and supply planning and matching activities. As illustrated in Exhibit 3-3, this includes segmenting customers based on buying criteria, controlling the flow of products through more traditional measures such as price, promotion, and placement of products based on availability, and collaboratively planning demand and supply throughout the Valueweb™.

The second value driver, coordinating the networked supply chain to meet customer fulfillment, focuses on the coordination of real-time order management and supply chain excellence. As illustrated in Exhibit 3-4, this includes providing delivery based on material, manufacturing, assembly, and transportation constraints, synchronizing execution, and replacing inventory with information.

The foundation for the networked supply chain (remember the supplier and customer communicators?) is the communication backbone. As shown in Exhibit 3-5, this com-

(text continues on page 66)

Exhibit 3-3. Value driver 1: influencing customer demand based on inventory visibility.

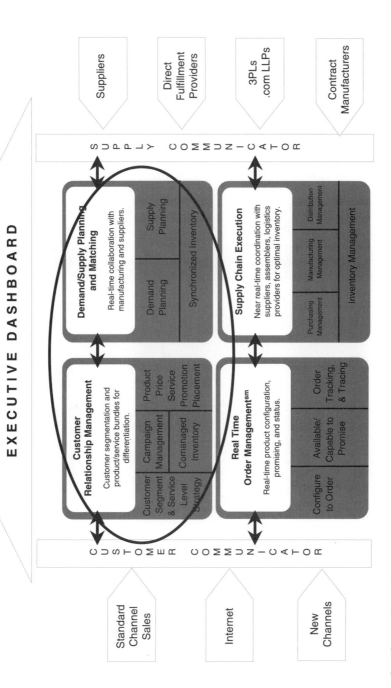

Source: Cap Gemini Ernst & Young.

Exhibit 3-4. Value driver 2: coordinating the networked supply chain to meet customer fulfillment.

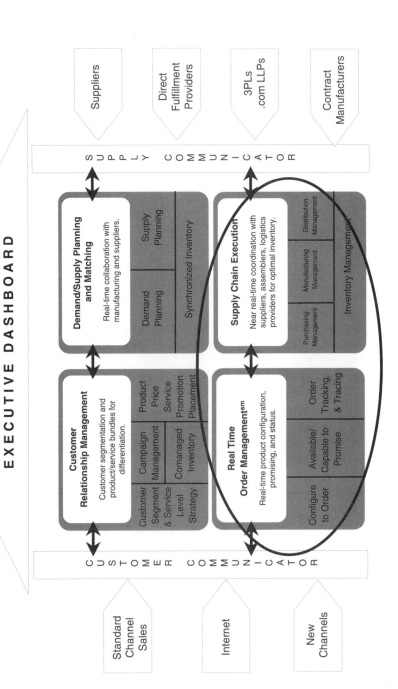

EXECUTIVE DASHBOARD

Customer Relationship Management
Customer segmentation and product/service bundles for differentiation.

| Customer Segment & Service Level Strategy | Campaign Management | Product Price Service Promotion Placement |
| | Comanaged Inventory | |

Demand/Supply Planning and Matching
Real-time collaboration with manufacturing and suppliers.

| Demand Planning | Supply Planning |
| Synchronized Inventory | |

Real Time Order Management℠
Real-time product configuration, promising, and status.

| Configure to Order | Available/ Capable to Promise | Order Tracking, & Tracing |

Supply Chain Execution
Near real-time coordination with suppliers, assemblers, logistics providers for optimal inventory.

| Purchasing Management | Manufacturing Management | Distribution Management |
| Inventory Management | | |

CUSTOMER CONNECTOR

SUPPLY CONNECTOR

Standard Channel Sales

Internet

New Channels

Suppliers

Direct Fulfillment Providers

3PLs .com LLPs

Contract Manufacturers

Source: Cap Gemini Ernst & Young.

Exhibit 3-5. Communication backbone: the foundation for networked supply chains.

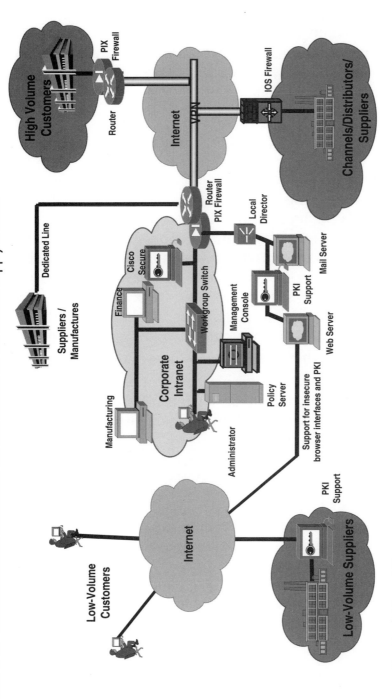

Source: Cap Gemini Ernst & Young.

munication backbone can lever Cisco Internet commerce technology to achieve global connectivity with appropriate security, reliability, and bandwidth availability. It is this communication foundation of the network architecture that allows for speed and connectivity between networked supply chain partners and enables collaboration.

WHERE ARE WE TODAY?

The small number of essential PC components has given rise to the outsourcing of assembly and shipping operations. However, given the limited supplier base for essential components, any shift in supply of essential components can create havoc in satisfying PC demand. It is obvious that integration and interoperability between assemblers, suppliers, and third party assemblers and logistics companies are critical to the success of any PC company in the near future. At the heart of this interoperability is the demand, supply, and supply chain planning across the extended enterprise value chain.

The CEO reflects on his own company within these market trends, and has mixed feelings. Progress has been made with his company, and the supply chain reengineering efforts have resulted in significant cost savings. Although he is proud of his efforts, he knows that this was just a start when compared with the upcoming world of the networked supply chain. He also notes a significant achievement in Texas.

Compaq Computer Corporation made significant strides in increasing its on-time delivery to its customers through reducing its order-to-receipt time. Compaq implemented i2's RHYTHM Demand Fulfillment module to gain available-to-promise (ATP) capability. Compaq is now able to start assembling a customer's order within two hours of its receipt.[5]

THE DELL DIRECT FACTOR

However, the CEO feels that there is another dark cloud hanging over his company. Deep in the heart of Texas, a company broke the rules of the game. Instead of a focus on earnings per share, this company focused on accelerated working capital turns. Instead of focusing on manufacturing efficiencies, this company focused on the customer. Instead of manufacturing for inventory, this company assembled product for specific customer orders and replaced inventory with information. From nowhere, this company ascended to a leadership position in high-tech personal computer hardware sales in the United States. This company is Dell Computer Corporation.

Dell started their company with a focus on customers. However, they took this focus and created a make-to-final customer order supply chain. The name for this supply chain model is now known as "the direct model" or the "Dell" model.[6]

At the time Dell initiated their model, the majority of personal computers and desktop computers were being sold through value-add resellers (VARs). These VARs quickly became very large and very numerous. Companies such as CompUSA, Circuit City, and Office Depot specialized in computer hardware and software sales to customers. Although these companies did, and still do, a fine job with their hardware and software sales, the VAR channel presented a three-pronged barrier of entry for Dell. First, larger computer manufacturers like Compaq and IBM already had a significant presence with each VAR. As such, shelf space would be difficult to attain. Second, the product life cycle of PC products was plummeting, with some products having life cycles of only three to six months. The potential for obsolescence was high, with products being produced in advance of sales to fill the VAR inventory pipeline. Third, cash flow for Dell during start-up was critical. It could ill-afford having its cash tied up in inventory (especially inventory at risk) in the VAR supply chain.

Why has Dell been such a factor in the industry? Direct connectivity to the customer is the primary reason. As stated earlier, the PC manufacturers have changed from direct innovation providers to indirect innovation providers. They are now driving toward customer ownership rather than innovation ownership.

The CEO of the high-tech hardware manufacturing company bought a Dell personal computer to track the Dell model firsthand. He had either read about or heard all the success stories, and was tired of having Dell steal his customers. He wanted to find out firsthand what the Dell direct model did for customer satisfaction.[7]

DELL'S ORDER-TO-DELIVERY PROCESS FIRSTHAND

The CEO secured a Dell brochure and called the 1-800 sales number. He easily walked through a few automated prompts that routed him to a desktop sales representative. His wait to speak to a live person was less than two minutes.

The desktop sales representative then asked the CEO his name, and what system he might be interested in purchasing. Although the CEO had already selected a system, the Dell representative asked questions about how the CEO would be using his new system. The Dell representative walked the CEO through a number of option selections that customized the system to the CEO's needs (for example, larger memory, an ISDN compatible modem, and a multipurpose printer with fax and copying capabilities).

The Dell representative even walked the CEO through the service help-desk procedures to be used for both system setup and service-related issues. The CEO bought the guaranteed twenty-four-hour service package that called for a replacement of the system if the problem is not fixed within twenty-four hours. In addition, the CEO was astonished to find out how advanced Dell's on-line service capability actually was versus the press release hype he was led to believe.

Throughout his discussions with the Dell representative, the CEO learned that some assembly and distribution of the

Dell computers are outsourced. The CEO determined that Dell is a sales and marketing company in the high-tech industry. There was a great difference between the Dell Direct model and his company. In his company, the pervasive mentality is manufacturing and engineering.

As mentioned earlier, the partial outsourcing of the assembly and distribution of Dell's computer products brings about a different set of challenges. These challenges are centered on complexity management. Demand planning, supply planning, and supply chain planning in a multicompany supply chain take on a significant complexity challenge. To do this with extremely short lead times (Dell promised the CEO delivery in three to five days) demands speed and intelligence in system solutions.

FIVE DRIVERS OF SHAREHOLDER VALUE—WORKING CAPITAL EFFICIENCY

The CEO had read about the negative working-capital potential for the Dell direct model. He found out about it firsthand. His credit card showed a transaction date for the day he ordered the personal computer. However, he received the PC three to five days later. Even if Dell paid their suppliers within thirty days, the free cash flow to Dell was significant.

Free cash flow is at the heart of the working-capital efficiency driver of shareholder value. This driver includes cash-to-cash cycle time, days of sales in inventory, inventory turns, days sales outstanding (accounts receivable), and days payables outstanding (accounts payables), as shown in Exhibit 3-6. Dell designed its make-to-final customer order supply chain model with direct connectivity to customer demand and working capital minimization as its two essential success factors.

The CEO also thought about his own philosophy. Supply chain velocity multiplied by margin equals power. Dell acceler-

Exhibit 3-6. The five drivers of shareholder value.

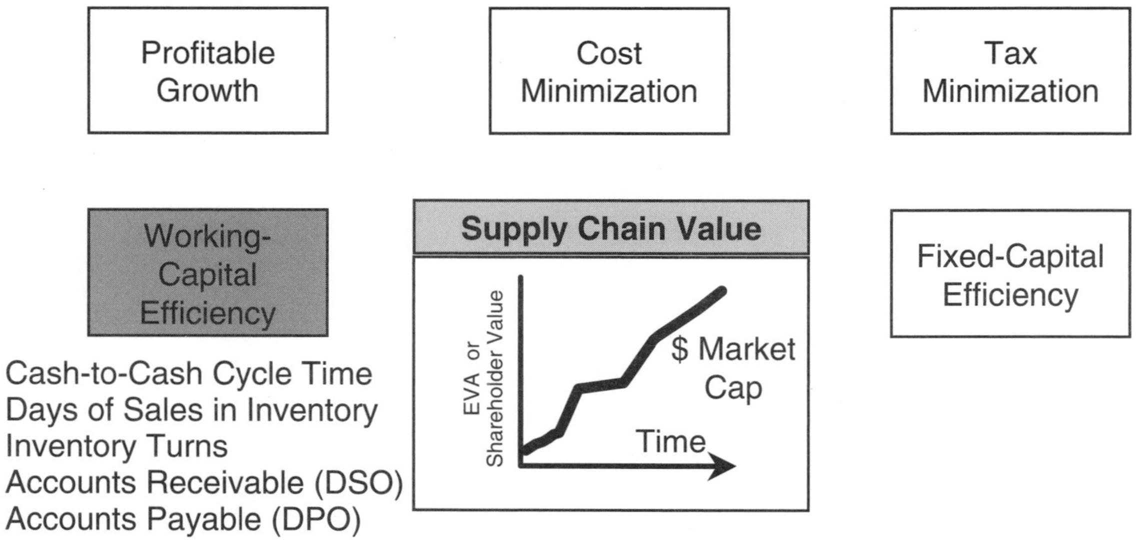

Profitable Growth	Cost Minimization	Tax Minimization

Working-Capital Efficiency	Supply Chain Value	Fixed-Capital Efficiency

Cash-to-Cash Cycle Time
Days of Sales in Inventory
Inventory Turns
Accounts Receivable (DSO)
Accounts Payable (DPO)

Supply Chain Value

$ Market Cap

EVA or Shareholder Value

Time

Source: Cap Gemini Ernst & Young.

ated the standard for supply chain velocity by going direct to final customers. Dell also expanded the standard for margins by eliminating the VAR from the supply chain and maximizing its working capital turns. As a result, Dell expanded its power in the PC industry in an accelerated manner.

THE CUSTOMER AND SUPPLIER CONNECTORS—THE HIGHTECHMATRIX™ CONNECTION

The communication backbone of the network architecture enables the customer and supplier connectors of the networked supply chain. This sounds fine, but what does it really do and how does it work?

There are two primary ways for a networked supply chain to be operational and effective. The first way is to enable a connection through the communicator that links "one to many." The second way is to create a private exchange or "hub" that has links to a much broader public exchange and other private exchange.

The HightechMatrix™ marketplace, illustrated in Exhibit 3-7, enables the networked supply chain. It is an intelligent business portal that connects one to many in the networked supply chain. Through this connection, the one has access to a plethora of value-add services that reside in a high-tech company, such as a PC manufacturer, or in the supplier and fulfillment service provider community, or in other networked supply chain participants, such as contract manufacturers or value-add retailers.

Through this technologically supported business portal, the networked supply chain can succeed like some of the world's best supply chains. It can focus all of the companies within the networked supply chain on the customer. Customers can access real-time information on inventory availability.

Exhibit 3-7. HighMatrix™ marketplace enabling networked supply chain.

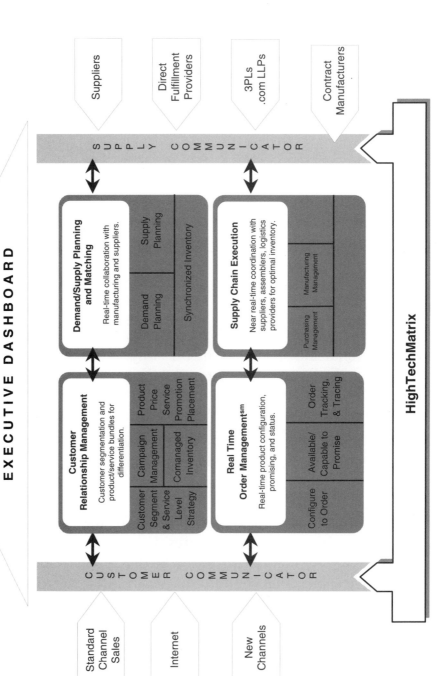

Source: Cap Gemini Ernst & Young.

They can use a front-end real-time order management system to configure their orders, secure a real-time promise to deliver, and receive delivery-tracking information, as shown in Exhibit 3-8. One customer, as such, has real-time access to the many supply chain companies that network together to fulfill product demand.

However, the real power of using the HightechMatrix with the networked supply chain process lies in its ability to create multivalue chain solutions. The PC manufacturer can have access to its suppliers and their designers of new products. Although the suppliers have assumed the lead role in direct product innovation in the PC industry, the PC manufacturers actually have the customer touch points. By combining the actual customer touch-point information with the designers of the PC components on a real-time basis, the innovation process can be brought to a new level—with Internet Speed.

There are numerous side benefits of using a Hightech-Matrix with the networked supply chain. For example, a PC manufacturer can have access to the acquisition of indirect materials in a pooling arrangement with other PC manufacturers through a neutral third party. In addition, PC manufacturers and value-add retailers can have access to an electronic private auction exchange to place PC inventory that has been reduced in value because of the release of a new generation of innovative product components.

WORKING CAPITAL EFFICIENCY— HOW TO GET STARTED

As mentioned earlier, there are three main areas of free cash flow and working-capital efficiency. These areas are inventory turns, days sales outstanding (accounts receivable), and days payable (accounts payable.) The executive must focus on business fundamentals to align these three areas to optimize free

Exhibit 3-8. Real-time order management.

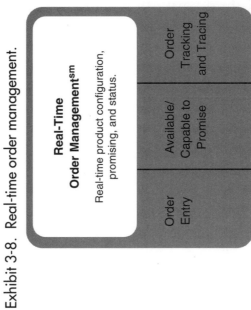

General Description:
An application that is the recipient and processor of orders exists as the order system of record. The application also provides an agreement to the customer that the company can provide the requested item by a promised date.

Interfaces with the customer to perform order planning, order generation and entry, order fulfillment, product configuration, order capture and commitment, and billing collection.

Driving Forces:
Need for the ability to verify customer demands and establishing realistic customer expectations (configuration and promise date).
Central repository for customer-placed orders.

Real-Time Order Management℠
Real-time product configuration, promising, and status.

| Order Entry | Available/ Capable to Promise | Order Tracking and Tracing |

Source: Cap Gemini Ernst & Young.

Working Capital Efficiency

Step 1: Identify, then institutionalize order-to-delivery expectations of customers.

Step 2: Establish customer payment parameters.

Step 3: Profile, then link order information visibility with suppliers.

Step 4: Map, then transform networked supply chain activities with compressed time-frame parameters.

Step 5: Establish supplier payment parameters.

---

cash flow. Here is a five-step process to get started on the road to greater working capital efficiency.

Step 1: Identify, then institutionalize order-to-delivery expectations of customers. Customers like to pay for items at the time of, or after, delivery. Customers also like to pay for expected service levels around consistent products. In the Dell example, Dell's consistent delivery within days of a customer placing an order allows it to receive the credit card charge at the time of delivery. The customer frequently pays his or her bill after the delivery of the PC or desktop computer. The result of compressing the time between the placement of the customer order and the delivery of the ordered product is the acceleration of the receivable "from order to cash." The two critical success factors here are speed and consistency.

Step 2: Establish customer-payment parameters. For PC companies that interact directly with customers, the establishment of customer-payment parameters is straightforward. There should be payment terms that stress cash or credit-card payments at the time the order is placed or at the time of delivery. Only account sales should be allowed. These accounts should be set up before orders are placed, and should be reserved for volume buyers. What about offering customers credit for their purchases? Credit is very dangerous with products that have life cycles that approximate payment terms. Our advice is to restrict credit sales to credit cards and to large-volume customers with known credit histories. If the computer, the price, and the service are overshadowed by the credit terms, then a corporate decision must be made about the profitability and risks associated with open credit terms. For nondirect distribution channels, tight credit terms are a necessity. Our advice is to treat the computer hardware as a perishable commodity, and get the money as close to the order date as possible. This will ensure better cash flow. It will also ensure better ordering habits by the retail or wholesale distributor.

One way to ensure customer satisfaction is to implement an on-line, real-time order management system with an interactive customer-order configurator. This allows the customer to be active in the product selection process as well as in their payment expectations.

Step 3: Profile, then link order information visibility with suppliers. The critical success factor in compressing customer orders for delivery/cash cycles is the immediate linkage of suppliers to actual customer orders. It is a simple fact that suppliers cannot fulfill actual customer demand without having the visibility of actual customer orders. The lack of visibility causes suppliers, wholesaler distributors, and even retailers to build up inventories to insulate themselves from the unknown fluctuations of customer demand. This distancing of the networked supply chain partners from the actual customer demand will encourage these partners to focus on internal efficiency activities instead of satisfying customer demand. These actions will add time between order and delivery, thus adding time between order and cash.

A critical activity here is to develop an electronic link between the real-time order management system, the bill of materials supporting the order configurator, and the suppliers. This electronic link from actual customer order to supplier bill of materials translates actual customer demand into "supplier speak." At the heart of this linkage are the customer and supplier communicators or portals. The selection of the portal provider should be based on connectivity to other processes in the networked supply chain.

Step 4: Map, then transform networked supply chain activities with compressed time-frame parameters. Once the information linkage is established (Step 3), the supply planning and supply chain planning activities should be performed. This effort should be done from raw materials to final product delivery. The competitive order-to-delivery customer expectations identified in Step 1 should guide the supply planning and supply chain activities. Realistic time parameters should be placed on each supply chain step. The executive should work backward, from delivery of the final product to shipping to assembly to component supply delivery, while mapping and setting strict time frames for each stage of the supply chain. Performance measurements and compensation plans should be aligned to reflect overall supply chain order-to-customer delivery execution and the individual functional performance (for example, assembly-to-ship time). The electronic link is to have the fulfillment process, complete with constraints, built into an order fulfillment system that is interactive with the real-time order management system. Customers can then understand real-world constraints when their products is configured, shipped, and delivered with a high degree of certainty.

Step 5: Establish supplier payment parameters. By compressing the time between customer order and product delivery, an executive is compressing the time between suppliers shipping materials or components and the customer providing the networked supply chain with the cash for the final product. Therefore, it is critical for the executive to align supplier payables, whenever possible, with final product customer delivery. Suppliers should be given incentives to manufacture according to actual customer demand. They should also be rewarded when this transformation occurs. Dell does not assemble and pay until a PC or desktop system is shipped to a customer. Saturn pays its customers once its cars are assembled. Once the payment process is designed with the appropriate rewards and penalties, the supply chain partners can function as one entity to access the customer cash as quickly as possible.

On-line order tracking through customer delivery is a necessary activity. It must be integrated into an automated payment system that is triggered by final customer delivery.

PULLING IT ALL TOGETHER

Identifying, then institutionalizing the customer order to delivery expectations sets the basis for supply chain time compression. It also provides entreé into establishing tight customer payment parameters. The supply chain partners must have access to actual customer demand if they are to have a sporting chance at fulfilling the customer's order-to-delivery time expectations. The networked supply chain must coordinate activities that both individually and collectively fit into the overall customer order-to-delivery time expectations. Included in this time coordination of activities are the alignment of performance measurements and compensation to reflect the performance of the networked supply chain as a whole and the individual's performance. An outcome of this process is delaying the value-add in the supply chain to as close to customer delivery as possible. This time compression also brings supplier payables closer to the customer's providing the networked supply chain with cash for the final product. Only the appropriate systems (Web-based and traditional) can accelerate the speed and accuracy of the flow of information from customer demand through the supply chain, customer delivery, and the cash transactions. Time compression and customer satisfaction mean cash acceleration.

The result of this process is compressed order-to-cash cycles, and includes faster receivables, compressed payables, and accelerated inventory turns. In other words, the result is accelerated working capital turns, greater free cash flow, and enhanced market capitalization. All shareholders of all supply chain partners benefit from this achievement.

SUMMARY: TIME WAITS FOR NO ONE

The CEO is excited but depressed. The marketplace advances in technology that could enhance his own company's customer-order-to-delivery process energize him. The connection to a networked supply chain represents a real opportunity for his company. It also is a huge change since he feels that his company is more oriented toward a linear, slower-moving supply chain.

The Dell direct process model and the rapid results that Dell enjoys with this model also energize him. However, he is slightly depressed because of the significant gap between his company and both the proven technology and the order-to-delivery process innovation in the marketplace. Moving to an e-business model that deals with both VARs and direct-to-customers can be difficult. The parallel paths can be constrained by traditional thinking, traditional organizational structures, traditional budgeting, distributor legal agreements, and a sheer lack of knowledge of "What's possible."

The migration to a networked supply chain that incorporates HightechMatrix as its technology-driven business portal appears to be one of the best ways to steer his company. He continues to ponder how he can transform his company using the Dell model while still meeting Wall Street's expectations on a quarter-to-quarter basis. The five-step process on how to get started provides an outline for beginning his efforts. One thing he knows for certain: He needs to get started or he will continue to be hammered by Wall Street.

In fact, as he ponders this again, a car goes by, and he curses his investment banker neighbor. He wishes he could start up a new company the way Dell did, and have a grace period from quarter-to-quarter pressures to build his own capability. He must do something, because time waits for no one—especially in the PC industry!

Whatever happened to the personal computer ordered by the CEO? His Dell PC arrived three days after he ordered it. To make matters worse, he had to wait in line to use it. His son had the computer up and running in less than an hour, and had already started playing games on it.

NOTES

1. "Standard & Poor's Industry Surveys: Computer Hardware," *Monthly Investment Review*, December 9, 1999, vol. 167, no. 49, sec. 2, p. 8.
2. Ibid, p. 1.
3. Ibid, p. 2.
4. Ibid, p. 18.
5. "High Tech Computers & Electronics," i2.com Web page, Compaq (http://i2.com/industries/community.cfm?industry_id=5&Story=65), pp. 1–3.
6. Michael Dell, *Direct from Dell* (New York: HarperCollins, 1999), p. 21.
7. Personal purchase by Fred A. Kuglin.

4

THE BIG WHEEL

KEEPS ON

TURNING

INTRODUCTION

It is 5:00 A.M., and the CEO is already in his office. It is a peaceful morning, with a fresh blanket of snow covering southern Michigan. The ride into the office was treacherous, even though he was driving his company's new sports car that has the next generation of brake systems. Snow, ice, and speed are not a positive mix for travel. The CEO's thoughts drift to a fateful January a couple of years before when a terrible snowstorm hit Detroit during the North American Auto Show. The foreign journalists attending the snow ripped the city of Detroit for its poor snow removal capability, and questioned why such a prestigious show continues to be held in Detroit. Senior executives in the industry quickly ascertained that snow removal is the least of the North American automotive industry's worries when it pertains to the global automotive industry.

NORTH AMERICAN AUTOMOTIVE INDUSTRY OVERVIEW

The North American automotive market is the largest market in the world. During the past several years, an economic boom in the United States has given rise to a steady market as well. Because of the market's size and the relative health of the economy in the United States over a prolonged period, the market has become a prime target for foreign automotive companies.

During the 1970s, foreign automotive manufacturers led by the big three Japanese nameplates targeted the North American small car market. During the 1980s, the foreign manufacturers targeted the mid-size car market. During the 1990s, the target became the North American luxury car market. In 1999,

Ford's Lincoln and General Motors' Cadillac divisions fell behind DaimlerChrysler's Mercedes-Benz brand and Toyota Motor Corp.'s Lexus division for the first time in the luxury segment. The year 1999 saw the targeting of the light truck market (minivans, sport utility vehicles, and lightweight commercial vehicles) by foreign manufacturers. In 1999, the automotive manufacturers based in the United States (including Chrysler, now part of DaimlerChrysler) accounted for 58.3 percent of the passenger cars sold in the United States and 81.3 percent of light-duty trucks. The loss in passenger cars to foreign competitors was 7.6 percentage points over a eleven-year period. The loss in light trucks accounted for 5.2 percentage points from 1996 to 1999 alone.[1]

What was troubling to most North American automotive industry executives were recent trends. Luxury cars and light-duty trucks (especially minivans and sport utility vehicles) are the most profitable market segments in North America. In addition, the North American market is the largest and most robust in the total global market.

GLOBAL MARKET CONCERNS

The European market, the second largest in the world, is a relatively mature automotive market. Europe continues to struggle under the weight of double-digit unemployment rates in its largest countries (such as in Germany and France). In addition, uncertainties about the political and economic impact of the Euro and the pending decision of Great Britain to join or not to join the EC are adding confusion to what we know as "Europe." However, perhaps the most confusing event is the potential political and economic reshuffling of Europe as it pertains to the addition of a dozen or more ex-Communist and other countries to the European Community. All of these events have combined to produce a slow growth forecast for automotive sales in the near term.

The Asian market is a double-edged sword for the automakers in the United States. The financial crisis that hit many Asian economies since 1997 has caused a reduction in domestic demand in most Asian countries. The impact on sales by the United States automakers in Asia was limited due to their small market penetration. However, the sales impact on the "big three" Japanese automakers was significant. In addition, the devaluation of the Yen and other Asian currencies to the dollar contributed to a significant cost advantage for Japanese transplants in the United States in terms of importation of parts for auto assembly. This situation was a contributor to prices being stable at the end of the 1990s and into the year 2000. In 1999, the combined North American car market share for Toyota (10.2 percent), Honda (9.8 percent), and Nissan (4.6 percent) was 24.7 percent.[2]

Our CEO reflected on these events surrounding the industry, but he is more troubled by a few different events. Several years ago, he spent time in Latin America as an expat in São Paulo, Brazil. This position was a key to his career path, because South America was the biggest profit-producing region for his company outside of the United States. At the center of this market was Brazil, which has approximately 166 million people. The CEO reflects that from the *real* plan of 1994 through roughly 1996, the demand for automobiles rose dramatically. After 1996, demand steadily softened until the devaluation of the *real* in 1999. Since the devaluation of the *real*, demand for automobiles in Brazil has plummeted. With Brazil being the dominant trading partner of the Mercosur trading bloc, the other countries of the Mercosur (notably Argentina, Uruguay, Paraguay, and Chile) have struggled immensely with their economies. When Brazil caught the flu, the rest of the Mercosur caught pneumonia.

With slow growth expected for both Europe and the rebounding economies of the Asian market, the plummeting automotive demand in Brazil and the Mercosur produces a distinct scenario for all automotive manufacturers. Worldwide demand for automobiles will continue to be exceeded by the worldwide capacity to produce automobiles. Simple supply and demand economics will dictate flat automobile prices in the foreseeable future. Given this fact, there will be increasing pressure to minimize costs, connect to actual customer demand, and leverage the fixed-asset infrastructures of the extended enterprises.

SUPPLY CHAIN CASE STUDY

Cost minimization is nothing new in the automotive industry. However, the use of constraint-based technology to improve process effectiveness is new. The CEO recalls a benchmark study that surfaced about technology-enabled process improvements involving Volvo Trucks North America. The numbers were smaller than his own, but this example paralleled the mass-customization challenges currently facing his own company.

Volvo Trucks wanted to manage its product variability and constraints to create an effective build schedule for its two production lines. Complicating matters was the inclusion of three manufacturing facilities into one build schedule, including the assembly facility, the paint and body facility, and the body-in-white facility. Perhaps the most imposing challenge was the paint and body facility. The paint shops are frequently the most prominent bottleneck in automotive assembly production. Integrating the paint shop schedule with the master build schedule represented a significant challenge that had tremendous upsides for Volvo.

(The CEO recalls his early days in an Asian country where the assembly operation was at continuous odds with the paint shop. The paint shop reported to someone other than him, even though he was the plant manager for assembly operations. The two had different build schedules, and frequently his plant ended up with white cars that had red or blue doors to assemble. The worst experience was the seven white cars produced with pink doors when the paint shop manager refused to take the proper time to clean the paint shop lines. Even the plant employees refused to drive the cars as demos!)

Using i2 Technologies' RHYTHM Sequencer, Volvo developed a solution for handling sequencing, material, and labor constraints. Volvo was able to expand the number of constraints considered in its scheduling process from twelve to fifteen up to seventy to eighty. In addition, material requirements are now tied to the schedule and passed along to operations, providing a single schedule for all three facilities. In addition, line-sequencing information is sent to many suppliers. This facilitates just-in-time deliveries for many parts.

According to James Sypniewski, the manager of business analysis at Volvo, success was easily measured: "Planning cycle time has been reduced from two days per line to just four hours for all lines. This allows us to integrate the company's manufacturing lines and supply chain with assurance that a balanced schedule will secure our industry-leading quality standard."[3]

Integrated assembly schedules incorporate customer-specific orders in a mass-production environment. This is exactly where the industry is heading from a process cost-minimization standpoint. Although the prospect of flat prices and intense competition are nothing new for the CEO, he hopes that using constraint-based technology tools will improve the effectiveness of the assembly process, as demonstrated in the Volvo example.

THE INTERNET AND THE CUSTOMER

The connection to customer demand is one area that keeps our CEO awake at night. There is one trend that totally consumes his attention. It is the use of the Internet by automotive consumers. Never before did consumers have access to so much information when purchasing an automobile. According to J.D. Powers and Associates, 25 percent of new vehicle buyers in 1998 used the Internet for assistance with their purchases. This number grew to 40 percent by the end of the first quarter of 1999. It predicted that by the end of the year 2000, the number would rise to 65 percent.[4] Consumers now have access to information such as dealer invoice amounts, car performance ratings, and even on-the-lot inventories of cars for numerous dealers.

However, an announcement by Toyota in mid-1999 really shook the industry. Toyota announced that it had developed a way to produce a car within five days of receiving a custom order. Security analysts believe this has a dual purpose—market share and connectivity to customer demand via the Internet. Historically, customers usually wait thirty to sixty days for custom-ordered cars. Daimler-Chrysler was generally believed to have the original standard in the industry with ten to twelve days. Toyota produces a "virtual production line" fifteen days in advance of production, and links the parts and systems requirements direct to suppliers. Actual custom orders are then added to the "virtual production line," with the provisional orders updated hourly to suppliers. Precise pick-ups from suppliers made by trucks running fixed routes, matched with hourly deliveries to assembly lines, support the Toyota five-day customer order program.[5]

As such, Toyota has designed a system that connects to customers ordering cars on the Internet or by other means and ships the cars within a best-in-class period. With automobile purchasing Web sites like Trilogy's carOrder.com, people can now order cars on-line with relative ease. The industry has made strides by allowing customers to search inventories of cars on-line for their car purchase. However, this only allows customers to look at cars already produced with specifications determined by the manufacturer. Toyota's program takes production to a new level by connecting to actual customer demand and shipping the desired car in less than a calendar week. At this time, it appears that Toyota is the industry leader in preparing their assembly operations to meet the emerging customer on-line demand and ship cars at Internet speed.

In addition to ordering new cars on the Internet, consumers have wide access to the pricing, terms, and availability of services around a new car purchase. These services cover financing, leasing options, extended warranties, trade-in allowances, insurance, and accessories. These services have always carried margins significantly higher than new car sales margins. As such, it is not only the new car margins that are under assault because of capacity exceeding demand and purchase information being plentiful but also the value-add accessories and services around the new cars.

The Internet is a potential disintermediation threat to dealers. Automotive dealers are somewhat protected by being legally connected to automotive original equipment manufacturers (OEMs) through their agreements. In addition, dealers have the customer touch points with consumers. However, automotive dealers have embraced the Internet in many ways.

AUTOLINK.COM

Autolink.com is a business-to-business Web site designed for automotive dealers. It provides on-line training for employees, customer relationship management services, mass-purchasing capabilities, automotive information services, and a specific e-mail capability for dealers.

The training services offer a learning center program designed to enhance a dealer's sales-staff competency in the areas of negotiating skills, selecting and presenting a vehicle, evaluating trade-ins, delivery, and follow-up with customers. With the high turnover of car sales professionals, these services help compress the time from hiring to sales effectiveness.

The customer relationship management programs help dealers shift funds from advertising to more effective one-to-one marketing techniques. This service also includes on-line service reminders, service appointment scheduling, and reporting.

The mass-purchasing capability allows dealers to pool their purchases and realize significant discounts on non-branded supplies and equipment. Examples are office supplies, service materials, and alternative sources for aftermarket replacement parts. In addition, dealers can order and pay for these supplies and equipment on-line.

Industry updates help consolidate current events in the industry for a one-stop review by dealers. In addition, the e-mail account helps facilitate communication between the dealers and their customers, colleagues, and suppliers.[6]

FIVE DRIVERS OF SHAREHOLDER VALUE— FIXED-CAPITAL EFFICIENCY

Since both cost minimization and connectivity to actual customer demand are being dramatically enhanced by technology, what about leveraging the fixed-asset infrastructure? The automotive industry has always been very capital-intensive. As illustrated in Exhibit 4-1, one of the five drivers of shareholder value is fixed-capital efficiency. Fixed-capital efficiency includes return on assets, network optimization, capacity management and throughput, and outsourcing noncritical asset-intensive functions. Two trends are critical to the leveraging of fixed-asset infrastructures: the world car and e-exchanges.

WORLD CAR AND E-EXCHANGES

Many people have attempted to produce a "world car." What most automotive manufacturers have succeeded in doing was to create reusable parts, subsystems, and systems in multiple-car platforms. For example, the Lincoln LS has multiple com-

Exhibit 4-1. The five drivers of shareholder value.

| Profitable Growth | Cost Minimization | Tax Minimization |

| Working-Capital Efficiency | Supply Chain Value | Fixed-Capital Efficiency |

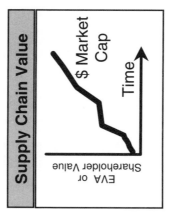

Supply Chain Value

$ Market Cap

Time

EVA or Shareholder Value

Return on Assets (PPE)
Network Optimization
Capacity Management/Throughput
Outsourcing

Source: Cap Gemini Ernst & Young.

ponents from the Jaguar car line. The Chevrolet Vectra in Brazil is virtually the same car as the Opal Vectra in Europe. The list goes on and on. However, what is really missing is the "world" in the world car.

One automotive manufacturer in Europe touts having a world car. However, the same car in South America has the same suppliers with the world car. The range of suppliers includes brake systems to water pumps. There are not that many brake-system suppliers in the world, and often it takes up to two years to develop a new brake system. However, water pumps are a commoditized part. Why wouldn't water pumps be sourced with local suppliers for the automotive production line? Importing water pumps from Europe to preserve the world-car design cost this particular automotive manufacturer approximately $40 per water pump. Assuming the production of 100,000 automobiles per plant, this amounts to $4 million! This amount was for only one part. How many other commoditized parts like a water pump are rigidly sourced through the world-car program?

Recently, there have been three announcements concerning e-exchanges, or e-marketplaces, involving the automotive industry. The two initial announcements were for exchanges with Ford Motor Company (Covisint) and General Motors Corporation (TradeXchange). These exchanges are focused on the purchasing of primarily indirect materials. In the future, it is hoped that they can be expanded into design and movement of parts, subsystems, and systems from tier-one, tier-two, and tier-three suppliers to the OEM assembly lines. The immediate benefit is to enable e-procurement, or the placement of many procurement activities on-line.

However, on February 25, 2000, General Motors Corporation, Ford Motor Corporation, and DaimlerChrysler AG announced that they would combine their purchasing efforts and create a combined on-line purchasing exchange. Analysts predict that this exchange will focus initially on indirect (noncar) parts and supplies, and evolve into car and truck parts. This combined exchange is intended to minimize the number of exchanges that suppliers work with. It also is designed for suppliers to use the system to gain process-operating efficiencies and to lower costs.[7] This industry-wide exchange is under review by the Federal Trade Commission of the United States government. However, just the fact that the "big three" automotive companies would get together to agree on an exchange shows strong support for the future of trading exchanges in the automotive industry.

E-Exchanges—Greater Value than Just E-Procurement?

The real value will be for these exchanges to transcend the transactional activities of procurement, and help automotive companies manage the complexities involved with the design and purchasing of the world car. For example, if an e-exchange used artificial intelligence and constraint-based technology, it could take into account the parameters of the two-year development cycle of brake systems, the plentiful nature of water-pump suppliers, the costs involved with importing items versus local sourcing of items, the local content rules involving countries where automobiles are assembled, and the form and features involved with alternative sources of products to produce optimal sourcing and design strategy for each adaptation of a world car. Therefore, whether this car was produced in France or Brazil, it would still be the same car. It would have a different set of suppliers with the same designs and different cost structures. Assuming this was attainable in the short term, the world car could even have a few local features that would make it more attractive to local markets and tastes.

What's Next?

Ford Motor Company and Trilogy Software Inc. are creating a separate joint venture for developing and operating all of

Ford's Web sites. These Web sites will focus on providing content and information for each of Ford's brands, including Ford, Lincoln, Mercury, Volvo, Jaguar, and Mazda. The target is existing car owners and new car purchasers.[8] It is obvious that customer retention and repeat purchases are at the heart of this joint venture with Ford.

Toyota Motor Corporation and i2 Technologies have announced a partnership to operate an electronic marketplace for the automotive replacement parts business. This partnership is called iStarXchange, and will serve the vehicle repair and maintenance industry.[9] There is potential to combine iStarXchange and Autolink.com in the future.

What we do know is that the automotive industry is moving at Internet speed. Information and business-to-business transactions will be Web-enabled, allowing for customers, manufacturers, suppliers, and dealers to thrive as they have never done so before. It could also spell the doom of many who ignore these trends and try to do business as they have done in the past.

We expect that major automotive companies will look to outside third-party logistics companies to function as a tier-one supplier for supply chain and logistics services on a global basis. Technology and the blurring of supply chains are moving so quickly that automotive companies will seek outside help to coordinate the brick-and-mortar and brick-and-click activities for their global supply chains. The key question is, Can leading third-party logistics companies break their traditional operating models and accept the challenge of being the e-supply chain provider for the major automotive OEMs?

WHAT'S NEXT? INNOVATION!

Our CEO is faced with an industry in which supply far exceeds demand and the consumer has instant access to information.

Using technology, the critical success factor for our CEO is to innovate. Innovation should be in two primary areas: business-to-consumer and business-to-business.

The business-to-consumer innovation must be centered around the consumer. We have covered a few examples where Toyota and Ford are actively trying to use Web-based technologies to gain access to the consumer. However, the next level of connectivity with the consumer involves the life cycle of the purchased car. Proactive maintenance reminders like what we saw in AutoLink.com, maintenance records that follow the car and do not disappear at the end of warranties, and owner preferences captured throughout touch points with the company are important next steps.

The big win will occur when automotive companies are able to integrate all the customer interactions into a customer lifecycle database. These interactions include the sales process, the repair and maintenance events, and the disposal or trade-in process for each vehicle. These interactions must include person-to-person touch points, paper touch points like customer satisfaction touch points, and electronic touch points. All customer touch points are important because they represent real customer satisfaction with the automotive company. This customer lifecycle database can be used not only to market existing cars but to feed the new product development process for developing new vehicles for the marketplace. This database can also be horizontally accessed for positive and negative preferences across a broad spectrum of customers. What better way is there to anchor new product development or adjustments to existing products than with the best customers?

The business-to-business innovation must involve more than merely automating existing processes. Let us take, for example, the area of containers. Containers are used to ship parts, subsystems, and systems from suppliers to automotive assembly plants. These containers are designed for specific car platforms and specific parts. For the most part, the majority of these containers do not represent a source of competitive advantage.

Some automotive companies treat returnable containers as assets, and others expense them. However, at any given point in time, the large automotive OEMs have hundreds of millions of dollars, if not billions, invested in returnable containers.

There has been some technology applied to balance containers from a central pool location (perhaps a third-party logistics company) to suppliers and automotive assembly plants on an as-needed basis. However, this only solves a short-term usage problem, and does very little to address the significant fixed-capital opportunity to effectively manage these assets.

Using technology to electronically house container designs can be a solid first step. These designs can then be accessed and reused as new car platforms are introduced. However, these containers must also be electronically tagged with a bar code or "license plate" and tracked from a central location. This electronic tracking can then be used to assess the numbers of containers versus the demand volume. Instead of pushing containers to or from suppliers and assembly plants, containers can be scheduled and pulled by the users as their parts, subsystems, and systems are shipped and delivered. The reusability of containers can help lower the design costs for containers. The tracking and scheduling of containers can dramatically lower the aggregate investment in these containers.

However, the big win is in the standardization of container designs used by multiple car companies. For example, a muffler supplier can ship virtually the same muffler to several automotive OEMs. The container does not represent a source of competitive advantage. Why can't the automotive industry use technology to design a standard container for mufflers for all OEMs to use? These containers can then be pooled on an *industry* basis, driving the aggregate numbers down and trips per container up significantly. These containers can even be designed with a common footprint to fit the standard shipping specifications for railcars and truck trailers. Perhaps combining technology with a little innovation can help the automotive industry to achieve savings in nine or ten figures.

FIXED CAPITAL EFFICIENCY—HOW TO GET STARTED

As stated earlier, the automotive industry is very capital-intensive. There are four main areas of fixed capital efficiency: return on assets, network optimization, capacity management and throughput, and outsourcing of noncritical asset-intensive functions. Here is a five-step process to get started on the road to greater fixed-capital efficiency.

Step 1: Identify existing and expected customer demand, then categorize by customer segment and product portfolio. The purpose of investing in fixed assets is to produce the products that customers demand. Fixed assets have operational and financial lives. The operational life of a fixed asset is tied to processes that support specific products. Therefore, existing

---

Fixed Capital Efficiency

Step 1: Identify existing and expected customer demand, then categorize by customer segment and product portfolio.

Step 2: Analyze network by product, by customer demand, and by financial analysis.

Step 3: Profile, then map demand to capacity by volume order-to-delivery time.

Step 4: Review outsourcing noncritical, asset-intensive activities—innovate!

and expected customer demand needs to be researched and tested on a continuing basis to ensure an alignment between the fixed assets supporting the products and the products themselves.

One way for automotive companies to get closer to customer demand is to create an interactive Web site to assist customers in their selection process; for example, the Ford/Trilogy joint venture. Many other automotive companies either have done this already or are contemplating a similar venture. However, the critical success factor is translating the collective learnings from their customer interactions into forecasted customer demand by products and by customer segments. The capturing of the customer preferences through on-line interactions (coupled with existing knowledge gained through dealer/ customer interactions) will help automotive companies to quickly adjust their product portfolios to customer preferences by customer segment. If the customer knowledge is only used to sell automobiles that are already built and sitting on a dealer lot, then the real value of the customer interactive Web site is lost. This knowledge must be incorporated into the *expected* customer demand and integrated into the production planning of the portfolio of products.

Step 2: Analyze network by product, customer demand, and financial analysis. The manufacturing and supply chain network infrastructure has a financial life as well. Plant and equipment is depreciated anywhere from five to twenty years, depending upon the asset. In the automotive world, very few car models have life cycles that reach five years, let alone twenty. The anticipated customer demand by product and by customer segment must be modeled for optimal utilization. The plant and logistics costs for each product must be known and modeled against the anticipated customer demand. The result of this network optimization must be rolled up into a capital appropriations plan that mirrors the sales and marketing plans for the product portfolio. As such, the interactive customer Web site should feed the sales and marketing plans and the capital appropriations plans on a continuous basis.

Step 3: Profile, then map demand-to-capacity by volume and by order-to-delivery time. The critical success factor in utilizing an optimized network is to allocate customer demand based on compressed order-to-delivery times (for example, Toyota's five-day order-to-ship program) and by cost. Production schedules should incorporate the changes in actual demand, and be integrated with suppliers and the networked supply chain. Flexibility is the critical success factor in this step. The production schedule should be fixed for the minimum amount of known customer demand. The production schedule and its associated processes should also be flexible to incorporate actual customer-demand changes secured from an interactive Web-ordering system. Using technology, an automotive company can take demand allocation and production capacity planning out of the boardroom and into the operations executives' hands—with increased effectiveness.

Step 4: Review outsourcing noncritical, asset-intensive activities—innovate! The return on net assets (RONA) follows a fundamental philosophy of investing. Investors provide resources for companies to acquire assets, and, in return, expect cash flows from the production and sales of products. Companies have core competencies. Honda, for example, is known for its core competency in engines. Toyota is known for its production system.

How many companies are known for having a core competency in the purchasing of indirect materials such as floor cleaning solvents, company travel, or telephone call slips? This is one major reason why automotive companies rushed to develop and outsource their indirect procurement exchanges as described in this chapter.

The automotive executives have been very aggressive in reviewing outsourcing alternatives for areas such as transportation. However, the use of technology has allowed the expansion of outsourcing options such as the tracking and processing of returnable containers. Executives should follow examples like this one to connect processes to achieve huge gains in leveraging fixed assets. An example of a connected process is the standardization of returnable containers across multiple car platforms, multiple divisions, and even multiple automotive OEMs. There could even be a returnable container e-exchange! Does the automotive executive really know when and where the returnable containers are at any given point in time? (Besides stacked up behind each automotive assembly plant?) What about the cost—regardless of capital versus expense—associated with containers? What about the benefits of design standardization across multiple divisions, matched with the on-line tracking of these containers? What about the benefits of standardization, then pooling with tier-one suppliers that supply multiple OEMs? With technology, the process benefits affecting fixed-capital efficiency are almost endless.

SUMMARY: PULLING IT ALL TOGETHER

The rush to set up interactive customer Web sites is a positive step for the automotive industry. However, the collective learnings from customer interactions must be captured and translated into forecasted customer demand by products and by customer segments for the real value of these Web sites to be realized. The adjustment of product portfolios to meet customer preferences creates additional value by reversing the forcing of customer demand into the existing products produced and sitting on lots. In addition, automotive executives must focus on customer lifecycle management.

Automotive executives should utilize enhanced network optimization systems and integrate them on-line with sales and marketing plans and capital appropriation plans to swiftly move their operations to meet actual customer demand. The allocation of this actual demand should focus on a fixed minimum as a base, then focus on maximum flexibility to incorporate Web-based orders. In addition, outsourcing should continuously be reviewed in areas previously ignored such as the design, tracking, and lifecycle management of returnable containers. The result should be the establishment and execution of a Web-enabled fixed-asset rationalization plan that is continuously linked to actual customer demand.

What cannot be lost in all of this is that results matter! From process cost reductions to customer-demand connectivity to fixed-asset leveraging, technology is helping to drive changes in this global industry. Change is happening at Internet speed, even in an industry that moves slower than the products they produce. Our CEO knows one thing—recent profit numbers will be hard to duplicate without help and a lot of change. Perhaps next year he can initiate the change, starting with hosting the North American Auto Show in Miami during January!

NOTES

1. *Ward's Automotive Reports*, January 10, 2000, pp. 1–10 and supplement.
2. Ibid.
3. "Volvo Trucks," Automotive & Industrial, the Community; i2.com Web Site, http://i2.com/industries/community.cfm?industry_id=2&Story=25, pp. 1–2.
4. "Standard & Poor's Industry Surveys: Autos and Auto Parts," *Monthly Investment Review*, December 9, 1999, vol. 167, no. 52, sec. 1, pp. 1–25.
5. Robert L. Simison, "Toyota Develops a Way to Make a Car Within Five Days of a Custom Order," *The Wall Street Journal*, August 1999, p. A3.
6. "What Is Autolink.com?" http://www.autolink.com/General Content/sitemapenl.htm, p.1
7. "Big 3 car makers plan online parts-purchasing exchange," Bloomberg News, *The Dallas Morning News*, February 26, 2000, p. 2F.

8. Alan Goldstein with Terry Bax, "Joint Venture by Ford, Trilogy to Enhance Consumer Web Sites," *The Dallas Morning News*, February 24, 2000, pp. D1, D3.

9. http://www.autolink.com/GeneralContent/sitemapenl.htm, op. cit.

5

LIFE AFTER

ERP?

INTRODUCTION

It is dusk, and the sky is crisp and clear on this autumn day. The brilliance of the setting sun contrasts sharply with the shades of blue in the sky. Soon the sky will be black, save for the light from the full moon. A helicopter has just lifted off from a mature, offshore well site deep in the Gulf of Mexico, near the coast of Louisiana. As his helicopter heads back to Houston, the CEO of a large oil and gas company who is on-board reflects on the sunset. He thinks of something that his father used to say, "Only God could make a sunset like that one!"

The CEO then reflects on the changes that have occurred in his industry during the past twenty years. The oil boom in the late 1970s and early 1980s, the oil bust in the late 1980s and into the 1990s, and the resurgence during the late 1990s caused a lot of turmoil in the industry. However, the sharp downturn in 1998 to 1999, followed by the equally sharp up-turn in late 1999, and the millennium year made everyone in the industry feel that they were on a roller-coaster ride. Break-even used to be $15 to $18 a barrel. Nowadays, his company could achieve a profit at $12 a barrel. Technology and reengin-eering for survival have combined to make the oil industry as competitive and efficient as it has ever been. The CEO thinks about the deep well that he has just left. Ten years ago, the well would have been written off as too expensive to drill, even though only 25 percent of its oil is being drained from the well. Today, with the use of horizontal drilling, he anticipates that his company will be able to recover from 50 to 75 percent of the total oil in the well.

During his college years, the CEO worked in the oil fields of Oklahoma. He remembers being an "oily" on the drilling rigs, and the difficulties of being part of a "wildcat" drilling company. His work took him to many fields, from far western Oklahoma through towns like Holdenville and Cushing to the far eastern edges of the state. Most of the oil wells dug in those days were traditional wells. He thought about the production of the wells, and how much more oil could have been drained from those wells if the current horizontal drilling technology had been available in those days.

INNOVATION

Horizontal drilling involves penetrating an oil well from a lateral angle instead of from a vertical one. Although this practice is rapidly gaining popularity in the oil exploration industry because of advances in technology, the practice itself is not new. The first patent for the precursor to horizontal drilling tools was issued in 1891, and the first horizontal well on record was drilled in 1929. The popularity of this method can be found in the results. Each horizontal well can produce from three to seven times more oil than a conventional vertical oil well.[1]

CONSOLIDATION IS RAMPANT

The oil industry has grown significantly since the CEO's early days. In fact, the oil industry is truly a global industry. As such, world events and megamergers continue to dominate the oil and gas industry landscape. To remain competitive amidst lower oil prices, several oil and oil-service companies have recently merged. These mergers include Mobil-Exxon, BP-Amoco, Seagull-Ocean Energy, Texaco-Monterey resources, Kerr-McGee-Oryx, Arco-Union Texas, Halliburton-Dresser Industries, Parker & Parsley-Mesa Petroleum, Sharpe Resources-Gulf Coast Oil, Sharpe resources-Aviva Petroleum, A2D Technologies-Interpretive Imaging, Weatherford International-Christina Companies, three Russian companies (Rosneft, Slavneft, Onako), Spanish Repsol and Argentine YPF,

French Total and Belgium's PetroFina, and possibly BP-Amoco and ARCO.[2] These megamergers of the late 1990s and the year 2000 would have made Mr. Rockefeller smile! However, the CEO wonders how much longer his company can remain in its present state, considering the consolidations and new competitive landscape created by these new megacompanies.

Imported Oil, Lobbying in Washington, and Global Ownership

The CEO also wonders about the current state of imported oil in the United States. He remembers the Arab Oil Embargo and the long gas lines at filling stations occurring when he was a college student in 1974. At that time, imported oil represented 36 percent of domestic consumption.[3] By January 1, 2000, the estimate was 56 percent. The U.S. Energy Department forecasts that the import percentage of domestic consumption will rise to 70 percent by the year 2020.[4]

The jury is out on the impact of imported oil on the United States economy. According to Mark P. Mills, senior fellow at the Competitive Enterprise Institute and coeditor of *The Power Report,* a newsletter published by Gilder Technology, the percentage of the gross domestic product for oil in the United States is approximately 30 percent lower than it was in 1990. Transportation uses two-thirds of all oil consumed, yet it represents only 10 percent of the United States economy. The other 90 percent of the economy get 55 percent of its energy from electricity. In addition, more than 80 percent of the growth in energy demand in the United States since 1990 has been met by electricity.[5]

Our CEO also thinks about his early days when he was a political lobbyist in Washington, D.C., and how difficult it must be for today's lobbyists. The political situation in the United States, he believes, is a catch-22. The average retail price for gasoline in 1998, when adjusted for inflation, was the lowest ever recorded. The average wellhead price for a barrel of oil was $10.88 in 1998.[6] This cheap oil contributed to massive budget deficits for oil-producing countries, and gave rise to economic decline and potential political unrest. Of the top-fifty oil and gas companies in the world, nineteen are completely state-owned and another nine have majority government ownership. Of the world's top twenty-five oil companies, fifteen are at least partly state-owned. He thinks about the top six oil-producing countries in the world (Saudi Arabia, the United States, Russia, Iran, China, and Venezuela), and recognizes only one, or possibly two, that have long-term prospects for political, economic, and social stability.[7]

The early part of the year 2000 witnessed the price per barrel of oil shooting up to an average of $28 to $32 per barrel. Cuts in production by the Organization of the Petroleum Exporting Countries (OPEC), higher demand in the United States, a resurgence of demand in Asia, and a reduction in production capacity from a decrease in capital spending during cheap oil days are combining to produce a supply-and-demand situation favorable for higher oil prices. The lack of predictability of the governments of many of top oil-producing countries gives rise to uncertainty as to whether production cuts will be maintained. As such, a catch-22 is created for political lobbyists. Cheap oil weakens existing independent companies in the United States such as his own, and contributes to acceleration of the import percentage of total consumption in the United States. Expensive oil causes inflation and slower economic growth, perhaps even a recession. Throw in the environmental issue of offshore drilling, and the situation looks complex, delicate, and confusing for lobbyists, Congress, and the public.

The political environment was never more volatile than in March 2000, when the United States pressured OPEC to increase production and lower the overall price per barrel of oil. Discussions reached a point where talk of military and other aid was mixed in with discussions about production quotas.

The result was announced by the Venezuelan oil minister and the new president of OPEC, Ali Rodriguez. Rodriguez stated that OPEC would increase oil output whenever the price of the cartel's oil exceeds $28 a barrel and lower output when the price dips below $22.[8]

The CEO has one important item that stays on top of his agenda. He must be a low-cost producer in the marketplace. This includes locating, extracting, and shipping crude from the ground through the pipeline to the first point of refining. Leveraging cost structures during times of volatile price swings must be the top priority for all oil and gas industry executives.

SHAREHOLDER VALUE: COST MINIMIZATION

Cost minimization is one of the five drivers of shareholder value, as illustrated in Exhibit 5-1. In today's volatile oil and gas industry, it is an essential driver for survival. Knowing one's costs across the supply chain is a solid first step for cost minimization. Having the right decision support systems for using ERP transactional data and minimizing the key cost components of the supply chain will differentiate winners from losers in the next decade. The goal is to use process cost reductions to minimize an item's total delivered costs to the final consumer. Reengineering on a continuous basis, sharing services with similar but noncompeting companies, and outsourcing of noncritical functions are all ways to minimize costs.

A quick benchmarking look at the industry shows some fine work in the standardization of common processes and software platforms in the finance area. Phillips Petroleum Company and Ultramar Diamond Shamrock (UDS) are two examples of successful SAP ERP implementations that have helped prepare their companies for common processes in the corporate finance area. This work also helped these companies make their systems Y2K compliant.[9]

Exhibit 5-1. The five drivers of shareholder value.

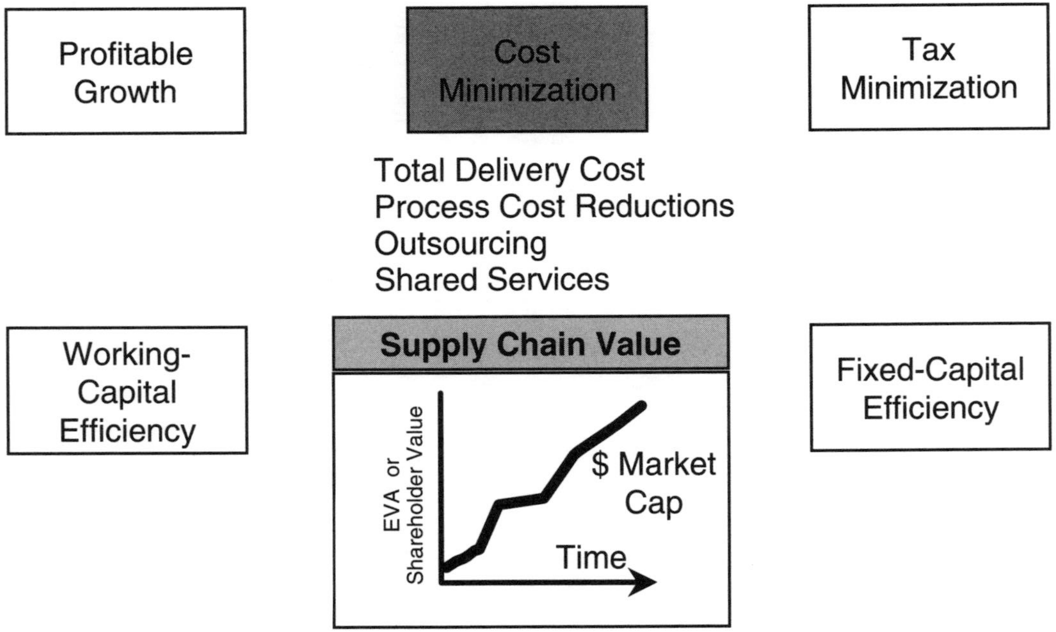

Tax
Minimization

Fixed-Capital
Efficiency

Profitable
Growth

Working-
Capital
Efficiency

Cost
Minimization

Total Delivery Cost
Process Cost Reductions
Outsourcing
Shared Services

Supply Chain Value

$ Market
Cap

Time

EVA or
Shareholder Value

Source: Cap Gemini Ernst & Young.

The CEO knows that he needs to take his company to a new level beyond ERP to compete in today's volatile environment. He needs to change his company into one that takes a more professional approach to supply-planning and demand fulfillment.

Another benchmarking effort involving a sister industry shows fine work by OxyChem, the chemical arm of Occidental Petroleum Company. OxyChem was faced with customer demands for higher levels of service, vendor-managed inventories, shorter lead times, and the demand for strict adherence to promised delivery times. OxyChem decided to support its reengineering effort with software that involved factory planning, supply chain planning, inventory planning, network optimization, and collaboration. These supporting systems were integrated with the SAP ERP system, enabling the ERP transactional data to be used for effective supply chain execution and supporting workflows.[10]

E-NERSECTION.COM

The benchmarking effort did uncover a Web-based start-up company designed to allow people in the oil and gas industry to procure equipment and supplies through the Internet. This start-up, e-Nersection.com, was created by W. J. "Zeke" Zeringue, a former president of Halliburton Energy Services, Inc., and a 1999 inductee into the Texas Tech Academy of Petroleum Engineering. Although the initial products and services appear to be basic in nature, Zeringue wants to focus on highly technical services in the oil and gas industry.[11] The innovation demonstrated by Zeringue with e-Nersection.com will be used by the team as a foundation for their spare-parts planning exchange.

DEMAND AND SUPPLY PLANNING

The consolidation of refining facilities and overall refining capacity in the United States has placed a tremendous amount of pressure on oil producers. The CEO's company now needs to manage capital investments in exploration and the supply of oil from existing and new wells. The balancing of the price per barrel of oil, the cost of extracting the oil, and the supply flows to meet the refinery demands are combining to drive the need for an e-based master plan. He needs the ERP execution of a Phillips Petroleum Company or UDS with decision support functionality similar to that realized by OxyChem. He decides to get his supply chain partners together to develop the right solution for his company within his specific industry segment.

The solution developed by the consortium of supply chain partners is to connect the demand planning of the refineries with the supply planning of the oil producers. Included in this connectivity is the creation of on-line demand fulfillment capabilities with oil pipeline companies, as illustrated in Exhibit 5-2.

Exhibit 5-2. Demand-and-supply fulfillment matching.

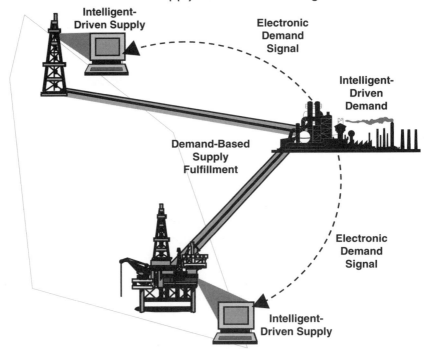

Source: Cap Gemini Ernst & Young.

An oil-field service company representative helps refine this solution even further. She convinces the CEO to add a spare-parts forecasting capability to the solution, connecting oil-field services companies to the CEO's company and his supply-planning master plan. The improved forecasting of spare-parts demand will translate into less oil well downtime and maximum production capability per oil well. The CEO sets out to design a private network of supply chain partners to aid his e-based master plan and spare-parts planning, such as the network illustrated in Exhibit 5-3.

Spare Parts Exchange—Cost Minimization and Supply Chain Solution

The plan is to enable the e-based spare-parts planning and master plan through a spare-parts e-exchange. This exchange would have three main components: procurement, commerce, and fulfillment.

The oil-field drilling and exploration equipment includes everything from the drilling rig to seismic computers to saltwater recovery equipment. It also includes nondrilling materials such as heavy-duty gloves, steel-toe shoes, cleaning solvents, and emergency aid kits. The procurement component of the spare-parts exchange will be connected to a data warehouse that stores the designs and specifications for all drilling equipment. Connected to this information will be the expected lifecycle of the equipment, the lead times for spare parts, and the original acquisition of the equipment by the oil exploration company. As such, all suppliers will need to be connected to use the services of this exchange.

The procurement component of the exchange will have an approved supplier setup process that includes everything from financial information to accounts payable/receivable agree-

Exhibit 5-3. Intelligence-driven supply chain.

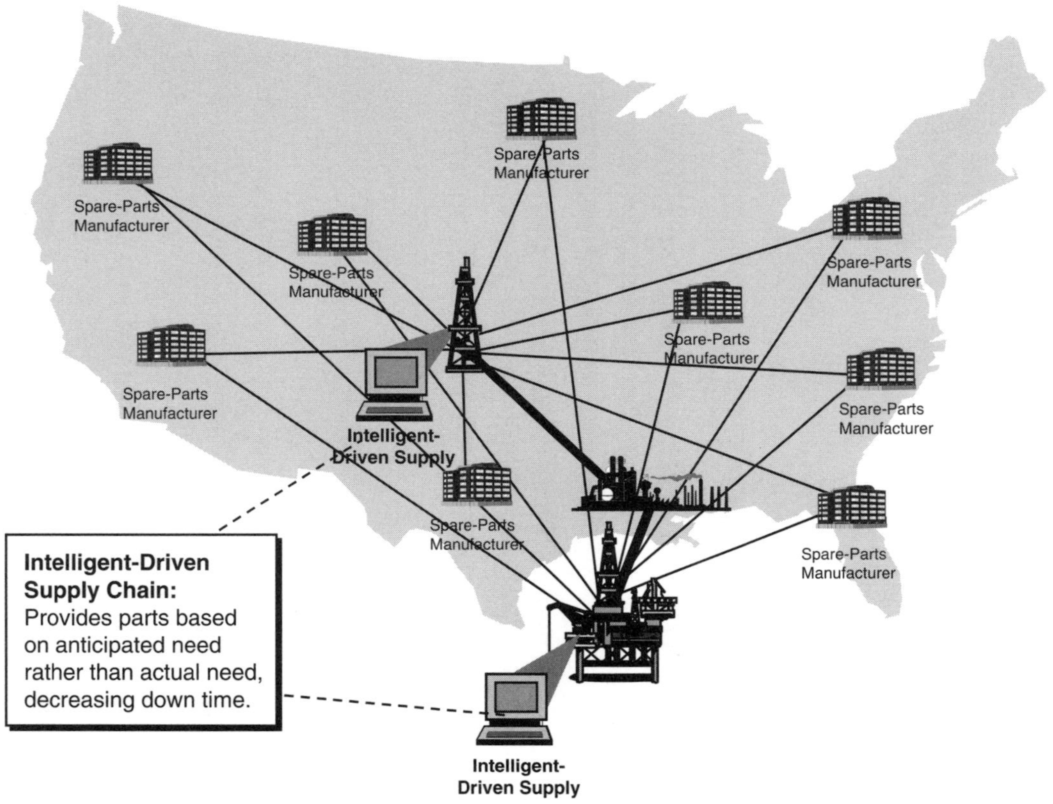

Spare-Parts Manufacturer

Spare-Parts Manufacturer

Spare-Parts Manufacturer

Spare-Parts Manufacturer

Spare-Parts Manufacturer

Spare-Parts Manufacturer

Spare-Parts Manufacturer

Spare-Parts Manufacturer

Spare-Parts Manufacturer

Intelligent-Driven Supply

Intelligent-Driven Supply

Intelligent-Driven Supply Chain: Provides parts based on anticipated need rather than actual need, decreasing down time.

Source: Cap Gemini Ernst & Young.

ments to contact names. Also included in the procurement component will be the warranties associated with original purchases, the master purchasing contracts covering specific suppliers of parts, and all approved suppliers for specific parts. All of these items will allow for on-line renewals of purchasing contracts. It will also allow approved suppliers to bid on any parts usage not covered by purchasing contracts.

The commerce component of the spare-parts exchange will be the execution component of the exchange. Parts can be either replacement parts under warranty, call-outs under master purchasing contracts, or open bids for noncontractual spot bids in an auction format. Regardless of the type of sale or trade, the commerce component will govern the offer parameters between the spare-parts suppliers and the oil exploration company. This electronic monitoring component, once established between the parties, will allow oil exploration companies to quickly acquire needed parts.

The administration of the sale will be connected to the commerce component of the exchange. The same information warehoused in the procurement component will be accessed by every offer transaction. This data will be used to execute purchase orders, invoices, and payments between the oil exploration company and the suppliers, thus eliminating invoice reconciliations and deductions. This process will allow the oil exploration company to spend more time exploring and drilling, and less time administrating the securing of these parts.

Perhaps the most critical component in this exchange will be the fulfillment component. The CEO reflects that every drilling rig that he has ever seen was rarely close to a major city. In addition, it is critical to minimize the downtime of a drilling rig. Therefore, the fulfillment component must address rapid response for rural and movable drilling sites.

The team creates a site-location Web site that inventories the exact location of every drilling site. This secured Web page includes drilling sites from all over the world. These site maps contain coordinates for offshore drilling sites, coordinates and topical maps for drilling sites in Saudi Arabia and Venezuela, and road signs with milepost markers and landmarks for land-based rural drilling sites. (The CEO thinks about the "Do Drop In" lounge in Holdenville that serves as a landmark at the major intersection in town. This lounge had excellent plate dinners for the oil-field services workers during the day, and had a bank of telephones for workers to coordinate their activities. It also served as the local knife and gun club in the evening. The CEO wonders whether the lounge has upscaled in the past few years and entered the "wired" world.)

The on-line buyers or drilling companies place orders with suppliers for specific drilling sites. The transportation and warehousing companies are linked to this information, and have connectivity right to the drilling site. The orders or offer are then attached to an available-to-promise commitment jointly by the supplier and the transportation provider. The drilling company can then plan his operations around the delivery date and the time that the spare parts are needed.

The real value of this exchange rests with its predictive demand-planning capability. By housing the original equipment acquisition and design information with historical performance information, the drilling company can then use intelligent e-business applications to forecast replacement needs. This information helps the suppliers to better balance their manufacturing schedules while focusing on satisfying routine maintenance and emergency repair requests. This predictive demand forecasting helps to lower manufacturing and transportation costs, and to enhance customer service. It also helps ensure greater up-time for drilling companies.

The e-based master plan and the spare parts exchange combined to produce an extended enterprise supply chain solution for the CEO's company. Not only can his company minimize the downtime of its drilling rigs, but it can better coordinate supply planning with the refinery demand forecast and the price per barrel of oil. His company can use innovations such as horizontal drilling to maximize production from specific well areas and link this expanded supply capacity to demand points around the world. The CEO can now use constraint-based decision support tools to know which wells to drill, in which areas to expand exploration, and which wells to cap while being completely integrated with his supply chain partners.

The spare parts exchange has additional potential for his company. Many spare-parts suppliers also use indirect materials for their own operations. Thus, the CEO's company can not only supply his oil-drilling teams with their indirect material needs but can supply his suppliers as well. This activity can help lower the fixed cost of the exchange itself, thus lowering the total landed cost of extracting oil from a well.

WHAT'S NEXT? MORE INNOVATION!

The upstream oil exploration business faces multiple challenges. As we have discussed, it is truly a global industry with supply and demand points all over the world. The supply of oil, its quality and landed cost (purchase plus transportation), the politics of OPEC, and the demand for oil combine to form a fairly complex set of scenarios for executives to optimize.

The long-term contracts, oil-futures trading, and spot-market trading must be linked to actual demand and refinery production capacity. The ability to have Web-based visibility for customer demand enhances global supply planning that takes into account previously identified constraints.

The Web-enhanced information sharing in the networked supply chain allows for concurrent planning across multiple supply chain partners. As demand is readjusted, the oil supply is reevaluated in terms of quantity, quality, delivery timing, and landed cost options. Efficient back-end decision support systems are a necessity to support the balancing of global supply with multirefinery production.

Another way to enhance innovation within the upstream oil industry is to connect its supply chain with the primary customers' supply chains. For example, the chemical industry is a multitrillion-dollar industry. The chemical industry has its own excess capacity, and is consistently looking for ways to sell excess inventory or excess production capacity. A trading exchange that is designed to assist oil exploration and trading companies to buy and sell petroleum can easily be modified to encompass spot trading and bidding for chemicals. Connecting these activities can even lead to integrated demand and supply planning by leveraging the information captured through the transactional activities. The result is a minimization of costs through the leveraging of technology-driven information infrastructures.

COST MINIMIZATION— HOW TO GET STARTED

For an oil and gas executive, the critical success factor is minimizing cost. There are many ways to approach cost reduction,

---

Cost Minimization

Step 1:   Know your costs.

Step 2:   Know your cost drivers.

Step 3:   Reengineer processes on a continuing basis.

Step 4:   Go straight to a pilot—avoid studies!

Step 5:   Push the line on innovation.

Step 6:   Review alternatives.

and several executives have done fine work in specific areas. A coordinated effort helps to jump-start cost-minimization efforts. The following is a six-step process to help an oil and gas executive to get started:

Step 1: Know your costs! To effectively reduce costs, an executive must know his or her real costs. These costs must accurately reflect the activities that occur across the supply chain. Whether it is activity-based costing or another costing system, there must be one consistent method of tracking and accounting for costs. The integrity of financial and operations reports is only as good as the numbers and what they represent. In addition, the decision support systems that support cost-reduction activities must rely on accurate numbers to produce valid outputs.

Step 2: Know your cost drivers! For every cost, there is a driving force behind it. Usually, these drivers are three-dimensional. The first dimension is the easiest one to grasp. A linear step function activity makes up the cost. For example, the pipeline transportation of oil or gas involves moving oil or gas from the well to a storage facility. This activity involves a series of pipelines networked together to facilitate this movement. There exists the cost of the pipeline infrastructure, the oil-well connection, the pipeline crossing, and the end storage activity. These linear costs are usually referred to in terms of cost-per-capacity utilization. As such, pipeline transportation companies try to maximize the throughput of the pipeline to leverage the fixed costs associated with it. The buffer in this case is either slowing down the oil extraction (or tanker unloading) process or increasing the oil inventories in storage.

The second dimension of a pipeline transportation cost is in terms of the cost per product measurement. This transportation cost can be measured in terms of cost per barrel or cost per BTU. This dimension allows for the leveraging of one cost to decrease a second cost component. For example, an oil refinery may be operating at maximum capacity for the grade of crude oil being shipped. The investment into intelligent pipeline monitoring and measurement systems linked into the production scheduling of the refinery can accelerate or divert the throughput of the pipeline on a "demand pull" basis. This will impact the pipeline's cost per unit shipped, but will lower the overall cost per refined oil products.

The third dimension of a transportation cost is in terms of customer service. Converting the entire networked supply chain into a cost-per-final oil product (for example, plastics or specialty chemicals) will break down the oil transported into final product groupings. This activity introduces multiple value-chain cost monitoring into traditional bulk-commodity aggregate cost components. The decisions impacting the flow of crude oil increase exponentially in this dimension, but so do the benefits. The specialty chemical business is in a severe overcapacity situation. Using intelligent e-business systems to collapse demand and supply planning across multiple value chains will ultimately reduce inventories of finished products. In an industry where margins are stressed due to capacity exceeding demand, any reductions in excess inventories are welcomed reductions in cost.

Step 3: Reengineer processes on a continuing basis. The three ways to measure costs as outlined in Step 2 need to come together to support an ongoing reengineering of the business processes. How do the three come together? The use of constraint-based modeling in a costing system, such as activity-based costing, helps multiple value-chain participants understand the various cost drivers in a networked supply chain. Consequently, multiple value-chain partners can make the right cost decisions functionally within their own enterprises and horizontally with their supply chain partners. These multidimensional cost-minimization decisions ensure customer connectivity and lead to profitable growth, fixed-asset leverage, working-capital leverage, and even tax minimization.

Step 4: Go straight to a pilot—avoid studies! Nothing sells like success. Use constraint-based modeling along with the correct cost accounting system to continuously reengineer business processes that have an emphasis on action. The output of constraint-based process modeling should be input directly into a pilot program for field-testing. Studies should be minimized or avoided when technology and accurate cost-accounting systems are combined to surface hard operational options for an executive team. The operational pilot should start by mapping out a scenario that encompasses at least two of the cost dimensions listed in Step 2. The executive team should find willing participants to put management time and resources into the pilot, and carefully monitor the pilot for proper results.

Step 5: Push the line on innovation. For those in the oil pipeline industry, do you remember the introduction of oil and gas flow measurement devices? It certainly sparked a fight with the traditional thinkers in the industry. Why did it take horizontal drilling so long to become popular in an industry desperate for productivity gains? In today's world, time waits for no one. The ability to use constraint-based technology to model process alternatives in a networked supply chain allows for the introduction of innovative ideas. The executive can visualize the results of innovative ideas (through new technologies that combine voice, graphics, and virtual reality) and accelerate the field-testing of the idea in a technology-enabled pilot.

Step 6: Review alternatives. Oil exploration companies have been very aggressive in exiting from certain steps in the oil and gas supply chains. However, there is a further opportunity for oil companies to share noncritical services with similar but noncompeting companies (an example of this is saltwater retention and recovery techniques). In addition, the traditional outsourcing of noncritical functions (such as data centers) is also a way to minimize costs.

SUMMARY

The oil exploration industry, despite appearing stodgy and slow, is actually a fast-moving and changing industry. Events surrounding the industry are giving rise to the incorporation of intelligent e-based solutions throughout the supply chains that support the industry. They are also giving rise to innovative ways to use Web-based technologies such as using a spare-parts exchange to minimize costs, create efficiencies in the supply chain, and drive shareholder value.

The CEO thinks about his recent trip to the Gulf of Mexico. Now that he has his solution plan in place, he decides to take his fishing gear on his next trip!

NOTES

1. "Oil & Gas Production & Marketing Industry Trends," vol. 167, no. 40, sec. 2, October 7, 1999, pp. 1–37.

2. A.F. Alhajji, "The Blight of Lower Oil Prices," *Alexander's Gas & Oil Connections*, vol. 4, issue 17, October 8, 1999, p. 7, http://www.gasandoil.com/goc/speeches/alhajji_2htm.

3. "Expensive Oil Is No Good for the U.S., Cheap Oil Even Worse," *Alexander's Gas & Oil Connections*, vol. 4, issue 17, October 8, 1999, p. 1, http://www.gasandoil.com/goc/news/ntn94156.htm.

4. Ibid.

5. Mark P. Mills, "Forget Oil. It's the Century of the Electron," *The Wall Street Journal*, February 23, 2000, p. A22.

6. "Oil & Gas Production & Marketing Industry Trends," pp. 1–37.

7. Ibid.

8. Associated Press, "OPEC Plans to Link Output with Price Range," *The Dallas Morning News*, April 1, 2000, P. 2F.

9. E&Y Marketing, "Corporate Systems Program at Phillips Petroleum Company and About Ultramar Diamond Shamrock (UDS)," Ernst & Young LLP success stories, Houston, January 2000.

10. "Helping OxyChem Create a World Class Supply Chain," i2 Technologies Web Page, Energy & Chemicals, The Community, pp. 1–2, http://www.i2.com/industries/community.cfm?industry_id = 3&story = 58.

11. Debra Beachy, "Many Workers Leaving Houston's Energy Industry for eCommerce," *The Dallas Morning News*, business sec., April 22, 2000, pp. 1F, 4F.

6

FROM 3PL TO

.COM LLP

INTRODUCTION

B ruce Jones sped down the highway with a growing sense of excitement. He was headed for his first day on the job as the new CEO of a prominent third-party logistics company, or 3PL. The retiring CEO, who had headed the company for the past ten years, had heavily recruited him for this position. Bruce had initially said no to the offer, but the offer kept getting sweeter and sweeter until it reached the point where it was impossible to refuse. He was now full of excitement and bursting with ideas about how to capitalize on the e-commerce revolution and bring his new company to previously unscaled heights of profitability.

Bruce had been the vice president of operations at one of the 3PL's largest clients. During the past few years, he had been encouraging and working with the 3PL to broaden its range of services. It was a win-win situation for both parties. His old company had been moving toward outsourcing more functions that were not part of its core competencies and wanted a strong outsourcing partner to work with. They had formed a partnership with the 3PL and had expanded the services that were outsourced.

The retiring CEO of the 3PL had developed great respect for Bruce and his understanding of the changing environment brought about by the Internet and its capabilities. He knew that Bruce was the right person to lead his company into the twenty-first century. Therefore, he refused to take no for an answer when he began recruiting Bruce for the position. From his perspective, the only problem was appeasing his client, Bruce's employer, from whom he was stealing Bruce. He convinced them that Bruce would still be heavily involved in servicing their account and since they were outsourcing many of Bruce's responsibilities anyway, this was a natural and advantageous move for all.

Negotiations had been successfully concluded, and Bruce was now headed for his first day on the job. His head was spinning with the possibilities open to them in the changing business environment. He was excited by the constant state of change and opportunities. Bruce also knew that he had to move quickly. From a personal perspective, he knew that there were very high expectations with respect to the company's performance under his leadership.

Bruce arrived at his office right on time and had a few hours to get situated in his new office before a 10:00 A.M. meeting that he had called for his executive staff. He had a good, experienced team in place, but Bruce knew that he would need to augment the staff with executives knowledgeable about information technology (IT). He knew that IT and the effective use of the Internet would be one of the keys to their future success.

Bruce began the meeting with introductions and words of assurance that this team was important to the company as they moved forward. He made it clear that no one's job was in jeopardy. The company was going to change and add significantly to its core services, but every service the company currently offered was still vitally important—as were its people. He then tried to impart his enthusiasm about the great opportunities that lay ahead and the challenges before them. He suggested a two-day off-site meeting to be held later that week at which to plot the future course of the company. In preparation for that meeting, he made some assignments. He wanted reports on the following four areas:

- The challenges facing the 3PL industry
- The emerging role of lead logistics providers (LLPs)
- The industry forces behind the LLPs
- Technology

His enthusiasm had been contagious. The members of the executive committee left the meeting with a sense of excitement and urgency that they had not felt in years. The business environment was changing as a result of the Internet, and they would be a vitally important part of that transformation. Each member began his or her tasks and prepared for the meeting in two days.

The two days passed quickly, and the executives gathered, ready to share their research and then plot a new strategy for the company. The reports began.

3PL Industry Challenges

One of the biggest challenges facing third-party logistics companies today is the blurring of value chains. This blurring is causing the 3PLs to focus more on value creation and less on reducing costs. This shift in the marketplace is causing tremendous stress on companies geared for cost reduction to change into one that creates value for its clients.

The CEO's 3PL had begun in a manner similar to most of its competitors. Its history was in providing basic transportation and warehousing services to clients. However, in recent years, its capabilities and services had expanded. Today, its services included:

- Direct transportation services
- Warehouse management
- Shipment consolidation
- Rate negotiation/carrier selection
- Freight payables
- Relabeling/repackaging
- Reverse logistics
- Order fulfillment
- Information technology

Bruce knew that his list of services was very traditional and focused on cost reduction. He also knew that in the world of the Internet, information had become an essential component and advanced information technology systems a requirement for gaining new business. Information was replacing inventory in supply chain management. This value driver was largely missing from his category of services. He knew that this last item was the key to his new company's future. It needed to help other companies transform from linear supply chains to networked supply chains, as illustrated in Exhibit 6-1.

THE EMERGING ROLE OF THE LEAD LOGISTICS PROVIDER (LLP)

The 3PL industry has net revenues of more than $13 billion per year, with the top twenty companies capturing almost $10 billion of the market, as listed in Exhibit 6-2. The companies have their roots in a variety of transportation and distribution-related businesses, including the following ones:

- Motor transportation
- Truck-leasing
- Warehouse operations
- Small-package delivery
- Air freight
- Air freight forwarding
- Ship lines
- Brokerage
- Manufacturing

The large 3PLs have Fortune 500 clients and now offer a range of services beyond their original roots. To varying degrees, each 3PL has recognized the value of information technology and has devoted significant resources to obtaining leading-edge

Exhibit 6-1. From linear supply chain to networked supply chain.

From Linear Supply Chain...

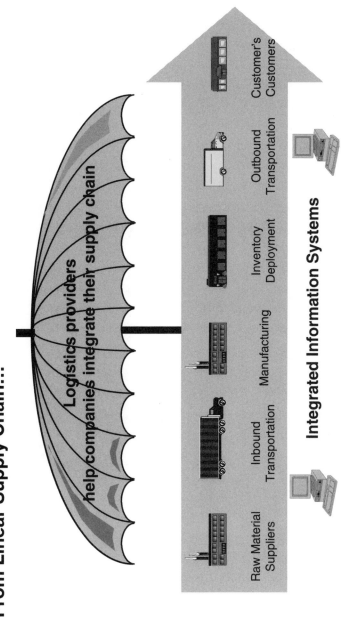

Logistics providers help companies integrate their supply chain

Raw Material Suppliers | Inbound Transportation | Manufacturing | Inventory Deployment | Outbound Transportation | Customer's Customers

Integrated Information Systems

(continues)

Exhibit 6-1 *(continued).*

...to Networked Supply Chain

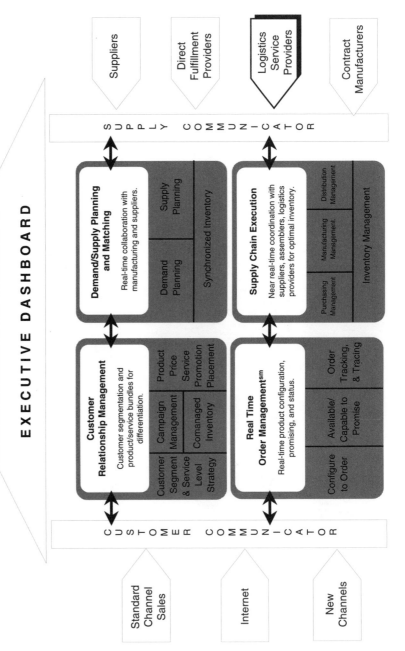

EXECUTIVE DASHBOARD

Customer Relationship Management
Customer segmentation and product/service bundles for differentiation.

Customer Segment & Service Level Strategy	Campaign Management	Product
	Comanaged Inventory	Price
		Service
		Promotion
		Placement

Demand/Supply Planning and Matching
Real-time collaboration with manufacturing and suppliers.

| Demand Planning | Supply Planning |
| Synchronized Inventory | |

Real Time Order Managementsm
Real-time product configuration, promising, and status.

| Configure to Order | Available/ Capable to Promise | Order Tracking, & Tracing |

Supply Chain Execution
Near real-time coordination with suppliers, assemblers, logistics providers for optimal inventory.

| Purchasing Management | Manufacturing Management. | Distribution Management |
| Inventory Management | | |

CUSTOMER COMMUNICATOR

SUPPLY COMMUNICATOR

Standard Channel Sales

Internet

New Channels

Suppliers

Direct Fulfillment Providers

Logistics Service Providers

Contract Manufacturers

Source: Cap Gemini Ernst & Young.

Exhibit 6-2. Top twenty 3PLs (U.S.–based, 1999) ($ in M).

3PL	Net Logistics Revenue	Gross Logistics Revenue
Ryder	1,287	1,713
Penske Logistics	959	1,133
Schneider Dedicated	875	875
Tibbett & Britten	659	659
Americold	650	650
North American	650	650
Fritz	578	1,388
UPS Logistics	488	757
Expeditors	442	1,445
USF Logistics	432	432
APL	420	420
CTI	382	484
Fed Ex	360	560
Menlo	358	716
Circle	332	814
JB Hunt Dedicated	320	320
Cat Logistics	317	317
GATX	294	294
C. H. Robinson	293	2,261
BAX	258	400

Gross revenues shown have not been reduced for purchased transportation costs. Net Logistics Revenues are better estimates of actual company activity and size.

Source: Armstrong & Associates, Inc., www.3plogistics.com/Financials.htm.

technology capabilities. However, despite their best intentions, the majority of 3PLs are still operating using the linear supply chains of their customers.

What is happening is that the market is driving the 3PLs into a new environment. This new class of service involves turning 3PLs into Lead Logistic Providers (LLPs). Whereas a 3PL provides outsourced services for a particular logistics function, an LLP provides an entire logistics solution for a company. For example, large automotive OEMs are giving tier-one suppliers the responsibility of coordinating parts from tier-three suppliers and subsystems from tier-two suppliers into complete systems. In the same way, several automotive OEMs are considering the establishment of an LLP to function as a tier-one supplier of global logistics services.

Whereas a large automotive OEM may contract with multiple 3PLs for various logistics services in various divisions, they would contract with only one LLP to serve the entire company. This LLP would then develop the overall logistics strategy, develop integrated logistics processes, provide software solutions, and subcontract to all other 3PLs as necessary. The transformation from a traditional 3PL into an LLP involves the following critical capabilities:

- The ability to provide strategic planning services
- The ability to provide operational scale
- The ability to provide financial scale (for example, freight payables globally)
- The ability to provide IT expertise to facilitate data flow and connectivity to the networked supply chain
- The ability to provide communications capabilities to networked supply chain partners anywhere around the globe[1]

These capabilities must take into account and encompass the forces driving change in the 3PL industry. The next report dealt with a description of the industry forces.

INDUSTRY FORCES FOR THE LLP

Because of the logistical complexities evolving in the twenty-first century, many companies, including Bruce's former employer, were waking to the realization that it was to their significant benefit to outsource their entire logistics functions. Their focus could then be on their core competencies. Among the challenges that companies and third-party logistics providers must face as LLPs are:

- *Globalization.* Companies must establish a multimodal network of carriers, freight forwarders, customs brokers, and financial institutions with global reach, while at the same time understanding the local requirements in each jurisdiction regarding taxes, customs/duties, and cultural requirements.

- *Mass customization.* Customers are demanding unique configuration, packaging, labeling, and shipping to meet their specific needs, while simultaneously demanding the simplicity and low cost associated with standardization. Although challenging to accomplish in one country, this becomes extremely challenging when applied to multiple countries (for example, the world car).

- *Real-time order tracking.* Customers want real-time information about order status and tracking. They not only want to have visibility about the shipment, but they also want to know if the shipment is deviating from its schedule. As dynamic scheduling becomes more mainstream with discrete global manufacturers, the reliance on up-to-the-minute information grows significantly.

- *The virtual, extended supply chain.* Logistics operations throughout the networked supply chain must be considered and optimized; considering the logistics needs of an individual company alone is no longer sufficient. The networked supply chain can only move as fast as its slowest moving partner.

- *E-commerce.* Fulfillment of e-commerce orders requires the shipment of small packages as opposed to the bulk shipments that most companies are best-equipped to handle. The challenge is to balance the efficiencies of bulk shipments with the individual on-line orders from customers. However, there is more to e-commerce logistics than merely fulfillment of small shipments. A Web-native approach involves load tendering, shipment optimization, shipment status, and freight/payment settlement. It is also about the alternative of providing these services in an Application Services Provider (ASP) environment.

⊕ *Reverse logistics.* Returns become a significant logistical issue in an e-commerce environment. In addition, the recycling of usable parts from returned products is increasing. Also, in industries where the environment and multiple governments are involved (for example, chemicals), reverse logistics plays an increasingly critical role (for example, electronic tracking of shipped chemicals, chemical containers, or the recovery of spent chemicals).

⊕ *Information systems/technology expense.* In order to operate an effective logistics operation, expensive information systems and technology are required. Information can replace inventory and result in significant savings, but only if the proper technology and systems are in place. Third-party logistics companies can provide technology leverage by pooling expensive technology for large groups of customers.

SHAREHOLDER VALUE—TAX MINIMIZATION

Tax minimization is one of the five drivers of shareholder value, as illustrated in Exhibit 6-3. In today's changing connected world, it is a critical driver for transformation success from a 3PL to a *.com*LLP. This is especially true in the global world of manufacturing.

Global tax issues become very important in making decisions regarding where to source and store product. The inclusion of tax considerations in network optimization planning can have a significant above- and below-the-line profit impact on most global companies. Networked supply chain decisions that position value-add activities in lower tax countries can save Global 200 companies upward of hundreds of millions of dollars. Tax minimization includes not only asset and sales lo-

Exhibit 6-3. The five drivers of shareholder value.

Profitable Growth

Cost Minimization

Tax Minimization

Asset and Sales Locations
Transfer Prices
Customs Duties
Commissionaire Structures

Working-Capital Efficiency

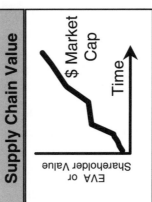

Supply Chain Value

$ Market Cap

Time

EVA or Shareholder Value

Fixed-Capital Efficiency

Source: Cap Gemini Ernst & Young.

cations, but transfer prices, customs duties, and commission-aire structures.

These were the types of challenges that Bruce intended to capitalize on to build his company's capabilities and make it the partner of choice as an LLP for many of the Fortune 500. His customers needed to transform themselves from companies into *.com*panies to capitalize on the Internet revolution. In helping them meet that challenge, Bruce knew that his company needed to transform itself from a 3PL into a *.com*LLP. His company needed to provide its customers with tools to replace inventory with information and to improve its responsiveness in serving its customers. Technology had to play a front and center role in his company's transformation process.

The final report of the morning focused on technology.

TECHNOLOGY: FROM 3PL TO *.com*LLP

The majority of large 3PLs offer a variety of services that are enabled by technology, such as:

- Inventory tracking
- Supplier management
- Carrier selection
- Route optimization
- Inbound shipment management
- Site selection
- Freight bill management
- Inbound/outbound/customs clearance
- Packaging/kitting/subassembly

The demands of a lead logistics partner grow into other more mainstream networked supply chain activities of a company. These activities are centered on end-to-end solutions, and include the following:

⊕ *Demand Planning.* Using a collaborative approach and sophisticated statistical modeling techniques, forecasting, and visibility into the demand projections of each customer by plant, division, and geographic region.

⊕ *Network Planning.* Development of a network strategy that meets customer service requirements at minimal cost by considering warehouse and hub locations, sourcing decisions, consolidation opportunities, merge-in-transit, and transportation mode options.

⊕ *Demand Fulfillment.* Capability that accounts for logistics in pricing and due-date quotes. The cost of transportation as well as relevant lead times are known and can be directly factored into customer quotes.

⊕ *Sourcing Strategy.* Factoring the cost of transportation into the procurement decision to ensure that sourcing decisions are based on purchasing plus logistics costs.

⊕ *Dynamic Sourcing.* Determining optimal sourcing decisions on a dynamic basis by considering customer service and lead time requirements as well as inventory, transportation, handling, and manufacturing costs.

⊕ *Capability to Deliver.* Given a due date and quote, determining the most cost-effective delivery mode.

⊕ *Status Tracking.* Monitoring all networked supply chain activity and notifying managers of problems.

⊕ *Reverse Logistics.* Planning the logistics of returned material.

⊕ *Contingency Planning.* Real-time planning of responses to exception situations.

After listening to reports on the industry challenges facing 3PLs, the emerging role of LLPs, and the industry forces behind LLPs and technology, Bruce thanked the presenters for their thorough analyses. However, there was one item missing from the presentation. In the networked supply chain, the supply communicator that electronically connects the 3PLs and

LLPs to the networked supply chain participants had not been clearly defined. He requested an analysis of how this supply communicator would be created.

TRANSPORTATION EXCHANGE—THE SUPPLY COMMUNICATOR

The emergence of transportation exchanges provides the link that connects the lead logistics providers and 3PLs to the networked supply chain. For example, i2, Ryder Logistics, and Central Transport International have formed a logistics industry marketplace called FreightMatrix™. Ryder is the anchor third-party logistics provider and Central Transportation International is the anchor motor carrier. The exchange offers shippers, carriers, and logistics providers the ability to buy and sell transportation through the exchange, plan their cargo requirements, and execute the delivery of shipments.[2] The exchange serves as a one-stop logistics provider for companies doing business with other i2 trading exchanges. From Ryder's perspective, the exchange gives them the opportunity to expand their customer base, reduce operational costs, and provide the necessary capabilities to become a large-scale LLP for Global 1000 clients. The Web-based access to networked supply solutions, such as demand and supply planning, provides Ryder the opportunity to become a *.com*LLP.

There seemed to be a variety of excellent reasons for Bruce's company to explore involvement in a transportation exchange like Ryder and Central, including

- Visibility to new customers and markets.
- Lower costs due to improved information flows. Using Internet workflow tools, shipment information such as freight tenders and bookings can be transferred between companies.

- Better customer service because of real-time visibility of shipment events.

- Reduction in payment cycle time because of an electronic funds transfer capability.

- Most important, the ability to transform the company from a traditional 3PL to a *.com*LLP!

OTHER SERVICES

Several days later, Bruce sat back in his office feeling very pleased about his first week on the job. The off-site meeting had been highly successful and generated many great ideas. The summary of the meeting had just been delivered to Bruce, and he was thinking about some of the essential ideas that had been generated.

- *E-fulfillment.* Companies are being challenged by the fulfillment end of their e-commerce business. Start-up companies typically focus on developing a great Web site and marketing their product. They do not have the skills, competencies, or infrastructure to deal with the fulfillment portion of the business. Therefore, they are looking at 3PLs to handle order fulfillment and delivery. This type of business provides many challenges since small quantities of stock keeping units (SKUs) from multiple vendors must be maintained, and then picked and shipped in quantities of ones and twos.

In addition to the start-up dot-coms, many traditional brick-and-mortar companies are also being challenged by the e-fulfillment needs of their e-commerce business. These companies are accustomed to shipping full pallets to large retailers and distributors. Their warehouses and logistics infrastructures are not set up to handle the e-business requirements of shipping small quantities to many customers. The group had recalled instances over the recent Christmas season when established retailers had failed miserably in fulfilling orders placed through their Web sites. Orders were not delivered before Christmas as promised, and customers were furious.

It is clear that 3PLs need to provide e-fulfillment services. The challenge for Bruce's company is how to accomplish this in an efficient, cost-effective manner. If they decide to focus on this area, they need to:

—Reconfigure their warehouses and install warehouse management software that would facilitate picking and shipping small orders and flow of goods information.

—Set up systems to commingle shipments from multiple vendors that are going to the same location.

—Develop delivery strategies to facilitate local delivery. Clearly, they would not set up the infrastructure to deliver directly to homes. However, other options included partnering with companies that offer local delivery services and/or local depots for customer pickup.

—Install systems that allow visibility of the order throughout the order fulfillment process so that customers have up-to-date information on the status of their order at all times.[3]

⊕ *Dynamic scheduling.* Using the right information technology (IT), they could go beyond tactical logistics to assist clients in designing their supply chain processes. This activity would replace inventory with information, improve their agility in meeting customer requirements, reduce cycle times, and improve customer service. Potential strategies that they could use to help clients implement dynamic scheduling include

—*Cross-Docking.* Product is moved directly from the receiving dock to the shipping dock without placing the product in storage. Cross-docking requires real-time communication and information from suppliers since the receiving function must know what is on a shipment before it arrives. Inventory is reduced because product is not stored; it simply flows through the warehouse.

Rather than each supplier shipping to each plant, shipments are made from multiple suppliers to multiple
plant destinations through a third-party consolidator, as
depicted in Exhibit 6-4. The automotive industry has
made significant use of 3PLs in managing their inbound
logistics network. Examples include:

- APL logistics will be handling inbound logistics
  for a new GM production plan in Thailand. They
  will manage the arrival of several thousand different parts per car arriving from various parts of
  Asia and Europe.[4]
- Burlington Air Express manages the inbound
  shipment of parts to GM factories in Europe, the
  Middle East, Africa, India, and the Americas.
  BAX is so integrated with the GM production
  schedule that to suppliers the distinction between the two is invisible.[5]
- Exel is managing a JIT inbound system for
  Daimler Chrysler. Exel receives electronic orders
  from Daimler Chrysler to pick up parts from suppliers in the southeastern United States. The
  parts are picked up, cross-docked, and consolidated for shipment to fifteen Daimler Chrysler
  assembly plants and arrive at the plant the next
  day.[6]

The value of an efficient inbound supply chain is not just
the cost savings that it realizes but also the significant
resultant increase in customer responsiveness. The
3PLs with the appropriate technology are instrumental
in helping to provide automobile manufacturers with
the ability to build cars to customer specifications more
quickly.

—*Merge-in-Transit.* Order components from suppliers are
brought together at a merge hub, consolidated, and then
shipped to customers. Because final consolidation takes

Exhibit 6-4. Accelerating network supply chain by simplifying complexity.

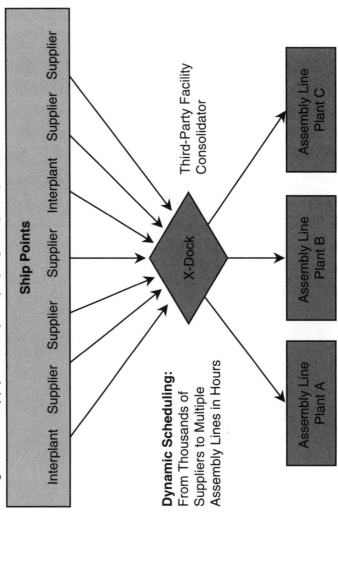

Ship Points

Interplant Supplier Supplier Interplant Supplier Supplier

Dynamic Scheduling:
From Thousands of
Suppliers to Multiple
Assembly Lines in Hours

X-Dock

Third-Party Facility
Consolidator

Assembly Line
Plant A

Assembly Line
Plant B

Assembly Line
Plant C

Source: Cap Gemini Ernst & Young.

place immediately before shipment to the customer and is based on known customer requirements, there is no need to maintain inventory of consolidated product.

—*Postponed Assembly.* Final assembly on a product occurs in the warehouse just before shipment to a customer based on the customer's specific requirements. Thus, inventory is reduced because the warehouse is not carrying an inventory of preconfigured products, only an inventory of the various components.

—*Delayed Allocation.* Inventory is allocated to a customer order at the last possible moment before final delivery. Product in the warehouse or in-transit is not allocated to an order until immediately before final delivery.

⊕ *Commingling.* Information technology architecture, tools, and methods can be deployed across clients so that loads can be maximized. Optimizing shipment of commingled loads across clients allows capacity to be shared and continuous moves to be maximized.[7] This results in savings for all and provides a competitive advantage to the 3PL in terms of pricing.

E-fulfillment is a *.com*LLP service that focuses on the business-to-consumer market. It is extremely competitive and time-sensitive. The previously-described activities are designed to help the *.com*LLP maintain full trucks, containers, and railcar loads throughout the networked supply chain, yet provide service to the consumer for the small quantities ordered. This is very difficult to do at Internet speed. Only the strongest will meet the increasing customer demands and thrive in this new era.

One area in which a *.com*LLP can gain a competitive advantage is the area of tax minimization. As mentioned earlier, a lead logistics provider that manages the global logistics activities for a global corporation has the opportunity to use the networked supply chain to drive a significant below-the-line tax-savings increase. Let us review how the senior executive of a *.com*LLP can get started in this service differentiator.

TAX MINIMIZATION—HOW TO GET STARTED

You read previously that global companies will increasingly rely on LLPs to handle the logistics of their businesses while they focus on their core competencies. In our global world, one of the key differentiators that an LLP can provide is its ability to consider tax implications, in addition to the other drivers of shareholder value, when setting up worldwide logistics networks and strategies. All the drivers of shareholder value come into play when developing a logistics strategy, but let us focus here on tax minimization as an important differentiator.

Step 1: Include tax implications in network analysis. The consideration of tax consequences when developing a logistics strategy can result in significant tax savings. A traditional network analysis looks to minimize costs and fixed- and working-capital investment while providing desired levels of customer service. This type of analysis deals with pretax profits. By also considering the tax implications of the logistics strategies, the worldwide effective tax rate can be minimized, resulting in maximization of overall profitability and shareholder value. The consideration of tax planning can provide significant impact not only globally but also in the United States, where local and state taxes can vary significantly by jurisdiction. An inte-

---

Tax Minimization

Step 1:   Include tax implications in network analysis.

Step 2:   Identify taxes impacted by supply chain decisions.

Step 3:   Review strategies for reducing taxes identified in Step 2.

Step 4:   Establish a centralized tax-planning model.

---

grated approach to logistics and tax planning ensures that operational cost savings will not be offset by an increase in taxes, but rather that the strategy adopted will minimize taxes within the operational framework.

Tax issues are complex and require the assistance of tax specialists to be effectively implemented. Following are a sampling of important focus areas and ideas to consider when addressing tax minimization.

Step 2: Identify taxes impacted by supply chain decisions. Consider two types of taxes: those that affect your profit-and-loss statement above the line and those that affect it below the line. The above-the-line taxes that can be impacted by supply chain decisions include

- Customs duties
- Value-added taxes (VAT)
- Sales/use taxes
- Excise taxes
- Property taxes
- Employment taxes
- Net worth/franchise taxes
- Incentives/credits

The *.com*LLP can reuse its tax database to its fullest potential once it is established. Of course, as in any knowledge object database, it is only as good as its inputs. It must be updated on a timely basis to be of value.

Step 3: Review strategies for reducing taxes identified in Step 2. Several strategies exist that can help reduce taxes impacted by supply chain decisions. Some of these strategies have been used for point savings, such as those from bonded warehousing. The critical success factor is to recognize the tax implications of the networked supply chain activities and incorporate them into the executive decision-making process. Here is a sample of some of these strategies:

⊕ *Bonded Warehousing and Foreign Trade Zones.* In this example, goods are stored in one country for ultimate distribution within that country or another country. An example of this is the free trade zone in Montevideo, Uruguay. The majority of the goods shipped into this free trade zone are for distribution to the larger Mercosur countries of Argentina and Brazil. The tax-savings opportunities involved with bonded warehousing and free trade zones include

—Avoidance/postponement of duty payments while goods are in storage

—No duty payments when goods are reexported

—Deferred payment schedules when goods are released

⊕ *Import Procedures and Taxable Value.* When goods are imported, the classification (duty rate) and customs value (taxable value) determine the amount of duties payable. Importation and/or exportation at previous stages of production can make duty reduction programs applicable. The critical success factor here is to move the value-added portion of the product to the lowest possible taxing country.

⊕ *Warehouse Location.* Within the United States, employment and property taxes vary significantly by location. These taxes must be considered when making warehouse location decisions. Although small compared to transportation costs, these costs may make a difference in warehouse location selections.

⊕ *United States Sales Tax.* The operating executives within the networked supply chain often overlook United States sales taxes. These taxes are smaller than many other supply chain cost components. However, in the right area, the proper management and structure of the operations can result in sales-tax savings. For example, the housing of company vehicles in a separate transportation company can reduce the sales taxes on transportation property.

Taxes that affect the below-the-line results of companies include the following:

—Federal income tax

—State income tax

—Foreign country income tax

These taxes must be understood and addressed on a holistic basis. There must be a convergence of the finance/tax departments and the supply chain operations departments to adequately take advantage of opportunities to lower tax liabilities.

Step 4: Establish a centralized tax-planning model. One method to consider in reducing below-the-line taxes is the centralized tax-planning model, as depicted in Exhibit 6-5. A supply chain management company is established to perform certain strategic supply chain management functions, such as supplier management and procurement, supply-demand planning, inventory management, and order management. It may also provide accounting, finance, and other shared-service functions. The supply chain management company is located and structured to have a low income tax rate. Once established, profits can be shifted to the supply chain management company where they are taxed at a lower rate. This rate is in comparison to other rates that may be in effect in other locations where sales and manufacturing activities take place. The supply chain management company provides a guaranteed market for production and incurs the inventory holding costs and risk associated with the sale. Under this model, profits are taxed at the supply chain management company.

SUMMARY

The previous scenarios provide some thoughts on tax minimization techniques that should be considered when making supply chain decisions. A key differentiator for a *.com*LLP is the

Exhibit 6-5. The supply chain management company.

Functions, risks, and profits are shifted to the Central Trading Company with a low effective tax rate.

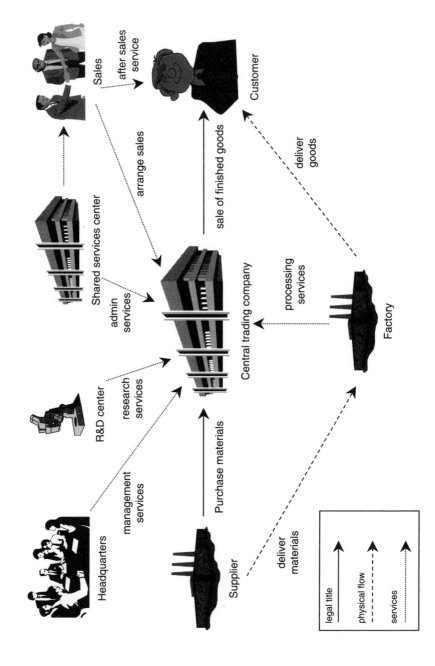

Source: Ernst & Young, LLP.

ability to team with an organization specializing in tax-effective supply chain management to assess tax impacts along with the other four drivers of shareholder value in making supply chain decisions. The benefit to companies will be two-fold. The discipline to review their own networked supply chains will produce infrastructure and operating savings. These savings are above-the-line savings. The review of the networked supply chain with tax minimization techniques will produce tax savings. These savings are above- and below-the-line savings. Combined, these total savings will have a significant impact to the bottom line of the clients of the *.com*LLP.

Completing his review, Bruce knew that he had made the right decision in joining the company and was excited about moving quickly to leverage the numerous opportunities in front of them. The key to their future success was the leveraging of technology to link into the networked supply chain of his customers. They could no longer operate as a traditional 3PL in their customers' linear supply chains. He also knew that the market was changing so fast that those companies that do not move quickly to capitalize on the opportunities might find themselves quickly out of business.

With the right processes, strategies, and technological tools, his company would become a *.com*LLP working with clients in an interconnected chain of *.com*panies. In today's Internet economy, it is not business as usual anymore with 3PLs.

Notes

1. Chris Newton, "You Should Expect More from Your 3PL," *The Report on Supply Chain Management,* April 1999, p. 9.
2. i2 press release, "i2 Expands TradeMatrix™ with Freight-Matrix™—Electronic Marketplace for Logistics Industry," February 29, 2000.
3. Stacie S. McCullough with Stan Dolberg, Liz Leyne, Andrew Reinhard, Jason Gatoff, "Mastering Commerce Logistics," *The Forrester Report,* August 1999, p. 8.

4. Dow Jones, "APL to Handle Logistics for GM's Thai Plant," *Business Times (Singapore)*, April 14, 1999.

5. "Burlington Air Express," *Who's Who in Logistics, Armstrong's Guide to Third Party Logistics Services Providers*, October 15, 1998.

6. "Exel Logistics," *Who's Who in Logistics: Armstrong's Guide to Third Party Logistics Services Providers*, October 15, 1998.

7. Beth Enslow, "Transportation and 3PL Providers: Invest in IT or Die," *Gartner,* March 5, 1999, p. 2.

7

FROM IDEA
TO LIFE

INTRODUCTION

Ted Crown, the CEO of a major pharmaceutical company, sat in his office in a state of despair. Just moments earlier, he had left a meeting at which Paulina Pearl, the vice president of research and development, had updated the executive committee about the status of their product development efforts. Developmental work on a new drug, on which they had placed so much hope, had to stop due to unfavorable results during phase III. They had devoted ten years and hundreds of millions of dollars to this drug's development, only to reach a dead end. Then, to make matters worse, Paulina reported that there were no major drugs in the pipeline that could become viable over the next one to two years, although there were several good candidates on the horizon in the next three to five years. The problem was that the patent on their best-selling drug would expire in two years, and they had been hoping that the drug that was just scrapped would have been able to make up for the loss in revenue when the patent expired.

THE IMPORTANCE OF RESEARCH AND DEVELOPMENT

The research and development (R&D) process is the lifeblood of their business. Patents on pharmaceutical products expire after seventeen years, opening the market to lower-cost generic products. Consequently, after the patent expires, there is a significant drop in sales of any given drug. Sales could drop off by as much as 80 percent after generic alternatives are introduced. Since 1984, when the Drug Price Competition and Patent Term Restoration Act was passed, the FDA has been able to quickly approve generic copies of brand-name drugs.[1] Thus, the time between patent expiration and the introduction of a generic alternative is minimal. Therefore, there is a constant need to introduce new products into the market to ensure the company's revenue stream. The drug development timeline is long and costly. A drug's development costs can exceed $500 million, and at any point in the process, it may be necessary to discontinue development. For every product that finally reaches the market, 5,000 to 10,000 compounds are screened, 250 enter preclinical testing, and five enter clinical testing. The entire process from idea to drug takes on average twelve to fifteen years.[2]

The top ten pharmaceutical companies each spend $1 billion to $3 billion in R&D annually, and the amount increases each year. Research-and-development expenditures by research-based pharmaceutical companies have more than doubled since 1990. In 2000, the percentage of sales allocated to R&D for research-based pharmaceutical companies is estimated at 20.3 percent. Compare that to 6.4 percent for electronics, 5.7 percent for telecommunications, and 3.7 percent for aerospace and defense. Clearly, the R&D expenditures by pharmaceutical companies on a percentage basis far exceed those of most other industries.[3]

RETURN ON INVESTMENT?

Considering the costs involved in developing a new drug, a 1994 study at Duke University revealed that only three out of every ten drug products introduced from 1980 to 1984 had returns that exceeded their after-tax R&D costs. In addition, 70 percent of a pharmaceutical company's sales were generated by 20 percent of its products.[4] Thus, it is extremely important to increase both the throughput and the success ratio of new drug products through a pharmaceutical company's R&D department.

As Ted thought about Paulina's presentation, he wondered about these statistics and why his own company had gotten itself into this predicament. The company was spending billions of dollars each year on product development, and yet its spending had been very ineffective. The company had also devoted a significant portion of its current budget to the new drug, which was now discontinued. Ted wondered to what extent they had even considered the probability of failure for this drug. It seemed that they had put many of their eggs in one basket, which had just come crashing down to the ground. He was very concerned about the process they were using to determine how to use those R&D dollars. He called Paulina and asked for a meeting the next day during which he wanted a review of their development portfolio and a discussion of how priorities were set and spending decisions made.

As Ted sat back and continued thinking through the implications of today's meeting, he realized that he needed to devise some strategies to ensure the profitability and success of his company over the next several years. He would address the product development issues tomorrow with Paulina, but for now he needed to address shorter-term strategies to ensure a positive cash flow for his company. He wanted to ensure that his company was operating as efficiently as possible. His company had been slow to adopt electronic commerce strategies, and he thought that perhaps these strategies might now become essential for ensuring his company's profitability. It is easy to ignore operational efficiency when you have a drug that is a cash cow and the money is streaming in. However, he knew that those days would soon end, and that he needed to pay more attention to the efficiency and effectiveness of the company's supply chain operations. He called his vice president of operations and suggested that they meet that afternoon.

ALLIANCES, MERGERS, AND ACQUISITIONS

Considering the long development cycle for pharmaceutical drugs, the only way for pharmaceutical companies to bridge the gaps between successful new products is through the acquisition of replacement products. The options are to quickly acquire a replacement for the drug they had just scrapped, to acquire a company with a strong and immediate new product pipeline, or to develop a strategic alliance.

Strategic alliances, mergers, and acquisitions are on the rise because of the cost pressures and shorter product life cycles being experienced by virtually all pharmaceutical companies. The number of strategic alliances in the industry increased five-fold from 1986 to 1998. Strategic alliances allow companies to copromote deals, expand product offerings by in-licensing them from other companies, and develop new biotech products through research collaboration with smaller companies. For example, a small biotech firm may be interested in an alliance with a large pharmaceutical company to obtain venture capital and a market presence. For example, Pfizer and Warner-Lambert collaborated on Lipitor, Pfizer and G.D. Searle on Celebrex, and Bristol-Myers Squibb and SmithKline Beecham on Avandia. With respect to mergers and acquisitions, these have also been on the rise since the mid-1980s. Some prominent examples are Hoechst AG/Rhone-Poulenc Rorer, Hoffmann-LaRoche/Boehringer Mannheim, Monsanto/Pharmacia, and Upjohn.[5]

THE NETWORKED SUPPLY CHAIN CONNECTION

Returning to his office, Ted prepared to meet with Steve Smith, his vice president of operations. Steve had only joined the firm two months earlier and was very anxious to introduce new technology and operating modes into the company. Steve had made a presentation several weeks ago on efficiencies that they could introduce into their networked supply chain. At that time, his reception from the executive committee had been lukewarm. When you have a steady stream of cash coming into a company, there is not much interest in gaining supply chain efficiencies. However, given the new turn of events and the potential slowdown in the inflow of cash in the near future, operational efficiencies would be needed to maintain the company's profitability. Additionally, operational efficiencies would free up cash that could potentially be used for additional R&D spending to speed up the development of their next blockbuster drug.

Steve had come to the company from the high-tech industry and was surprised to find a low level of supply chain technology adaptation there. After networking within the industry, he found that this was the norm. Much of the focus over the last few years had been on installing ERP and dealing with Y2K issues. He believed that there was now tremendous opportunity to move forward with certain technology projects that could yield significant benefits in terms of taking costs out of the supply chain. First, he felt that the company needed to focus on streamlining and achieving efficiencies in internal operations. Secondly, he was hopeful that the company would become involved in leveraging the capabilities of the Internet.

With respect to internal operations, Steve found that the company maintained a large amount of inventory in its pipeline. Although customer service requirements were high, the amount of raw, work-in-process, and finished goods inventory in the pipeline was significantly higher than would be required if the supply chain was well-managed. Steve felt that there was significant opportunity to free up dollars currently invested in working capital. However, to free up those inventory dollars while maintaining high customer service levels, some investment would be required in state-of-the-art networked supply chain management systems. The software would help the company to better anticipate demand and then to produce and position inventory effectively to meet that demand. These systems include demand planning, supply planning, supply chain planning, and demand fulfillment. Putting these systems in place would require some investment, but the payback would be significant.

TECHNOLOGY WITH NETWORKED SUPPLY CHAIN ALLIANCE PARTNERS

Steve then turned his discussion to the Internet and the concept of trading exchanges—communities on the Internet where goods, services, and information are exchanged among multiple partners. Although these concepts were new in the industry, Steve quoted *Forrester*'s prediction that 17 percent of business-to-business health-care trade will occur on the Internet by 2004.[6] This move to the Internet would be driven by the need of all parties involved in the supply chain to reduce costs. Therefore, the entire supply chain could dramatically change into a networked supply chain.

Steve felt that there were opportunities for them to buy as well as sell on the Internet. On the buying side, there was an opportunity to lower administrative as well as purchase costs and to have access to a broader range of suppliers. On the supply side, there were various exchanges involving wholesalers, distributors, buying groups, drug chains, and Internet pharmacies where they could make their products available for sale. However, to effectively sell products on a Web site, it was not enough to merely offer product and price availability on-line. The value of the Internet, and the way that they could differentiate themselves, would be for them to provide the buyer with on-line access to information on product availability and delivery dates. To achieve these capabilities, they first needed to have their in-house supply chain systems operating effectively and linked to the Web sites to provide real-time information on inventory availability and production capacities. Linking with their customers would also provide opportunities for collaboratively planning and forecasting.

Ted was impressed by the presentation and gave Steve the okay to proceed to the next step and begin bringing in software vendors and consultants to start the process of upgrading their supply chain systems and processes so that they could then start to leverage the opportunities available on the Internet. The opportunity was there to generate much-needed cash by optimizing their supply chain and linking in with their suppliers and customers.

BACK TO R&D—THE HEARTBEAT OF PHARMACEUTICAL COMPANIES

Despite the unique characteristics of an R&D department, it should have disciplines and processes to guide its efficiencies and effectiveness. The product portfolio of an R&D department should be professionally managed according to these disciplines and processes. Let us look at this approach with Paulina and Ted.

The next morning, Paulina arrived at Ted's office promptly at 8:00 A.M. armed with stacks of reports and several of the people who were leading some essential R&D projects. She began her presentation by discussing the multiple drug candidates currently under development. She presented the project plan and cost tracking for each. The individuals she brought with her each spoke eloquently about the importance of the efforts that they were leading. Paulina then began a pitch for more R&D funding, indicating that there were insufficient funds in the budget to proceed with all the drug candidates in their portfolio based on the project plans she had presented. She discussed the importance of the R&D efforts and indicated that if they had more funds they could have moved more quickly with certain projects and the company would not be in its current situation of having no blockbuster drug to introduce for the next several years. She came prepared with a budget request for an annual 20 percent increase in funding.

This was not the answer that Ted was looking for. Although he certainly understood the importance of R&D spending, in their current situation of limited cash flow over the next few years, the last thing he wanted to do was to increase spending. Their R&D budget was already quite substantial. He wanted to know how they could use the current budget more effectively, not how to spend more money. They needed to optimize the utilization of their assets.

Ted starting asking questions about priorities. He understood that there was insufficient budget to proceed quickly on all projects. His concern was how the money was being allocated. Which projects moved forward when there were scarce resources? How were the decisions made? He listened to the project managers that Paulina had brought to the meeting and one thing become clear: Each was defending his or her own project; not one was looking at the big picture. Through the discussion, it became clear that resource-allocation decisions were being made based on power relationships and in-fighting compromise. Ted felt that one of the issues that had brought them to their current situation was a lack of understanding of the risk in the various projects and for the portfolio overall. When he raised this issue, the responses went back to vehement support by each of the project managers for his or her particular project versus an overall understanding of the risk profile of the company.

After a few hours of discussion, Ted asked the project managers to leave and for Paulina to remain. He told her that he was unhappy with the way the company's portfolio was being managed, that there would be no budget increase, and that he expected her to develop processes that allowed them to use their existing budget more effectively. The large stack of reports sitting on the table in front of her was focused on cost and activity tracking. He wanted to shift the focus to optimizing schedules and maximizing the effectiveness of resource utilization. Her department needed to understand that the ultimate goal is profit maximization, which entailed investing their money in the most efficient manner to optimize revenue.

On the basis of that morning's discussion, Tad told Paulina that he had identified the following issues that he wanted her to fix:

- Decisions about how to allocate scarce resources are being made based on company politics rather than on a fact-based analysis that balances technical success with commercial attractiveness.

- There is no regard to capacity constraints. Individual project work plans are developed assuming infinite capacity.

- There is no quick go/no go decision-making process to kill low-value projects before they use valuable resources.

- Aggregate portfolio risk is not being assessed.

- Goals and performance metrics encourage project managers to be concerned only with the success of their own particular projects rather than encouraging an interest in the success of the overall company portfolio.

Paulina agreed that all of the issues Ted had identified were indeed problems. Some were organizational and process issues that she could address. Others, however, required a technology infrastructure that the company did not have. The project management tools that they were currently using emphasized unconstrained planning and had no optimization capabilities. If Ted were committed to changing the way the company managed its portfolio and developed schedules, they would need a new process with new technology.

PRODUCT LIFECYCLE MANAGEMENT

Seven days later, after an exhausting week, Paulina returned to Ted's office. She had done extensive research and was prepared to discuss with Ted a technological approach that she had found, called product lifecycle management (PLM). She felt that this approach would significantly aid the company in managing its R&D expenditures. As she explained to Ted, two highly integrated processes need to work together.

1. *Portfolio Planning* selects alternatives and prioritizes projects.

2. *Development Scheduling* manages resources and optimizes velocity and throughput for those projects selected and prioritized in the portfolio-planning process.

The critical success factor for both of these processes is the gathering of the appropriate data, as depicted in Exhibit 7-1. There are four groups of data that need to be gathered for these processes. These groups are project-planning inputs, resource inputs, financial inputs, and market intelligence inputs. These groups of data become inputs into the processes and the technology supporting portfolio planning and development scheduling. The project-planning inputs include the active project phase, the task duration, the task dependencies, and the assessed probability of success by phase. The resource inputs are the resource requirements and availability to support the project tasks throughout the project's duration. The financial inputs are the resource costs, the overall development costs, the estimated production costs, and the anticipated selling prices for the drug products under development. The market intelligence inputs are the estimated market size and the expected market share for the new drug under development.

The new product development portfolio is developed considering these inputs along with the company's strategic direction, for example, the priority of development in selected therapeutic classes. Then the most effective new product portfolio is developed and prioritized. This information, along with the detailed inputs described above, are then used to develop constrained development schedules that take into account the availability of resources and allocate those resources to their highest valued usage. The system identifies bottlenecks so that decisions can be made about adding resources in selected areas and then helps to identify the actual benefit of adding those resources.

Exhibit 7-1. Product life cycle management.

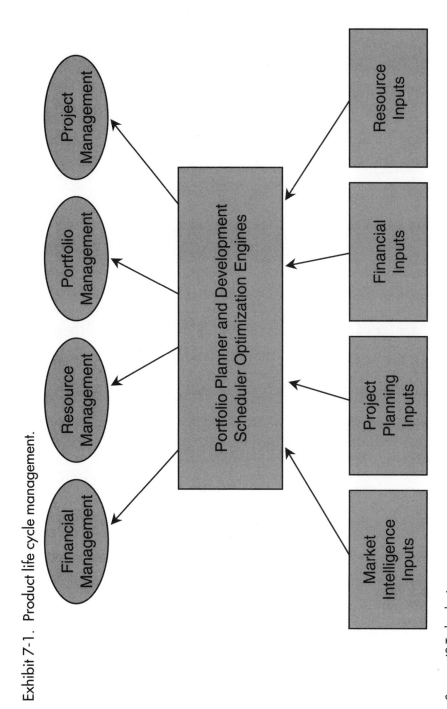

Source: i2 Technologies.

Overall, the new process and system accomplished exactly what Ted had been looking for

- Maximization of portfolio profitability
- Acceleration of high-margin projects
- Rapid termination of low-value projects
- Increased development throughput
- Streamlined research-and-development process
- Quicker response to opportunities and threats

Given this structured approach, resources would no longer be allocated based on the influence or seniority of the project manager, but rather on the impact that the investment would ultimately have on the profitability of the company. As depicted in Exhibit 7-2, this system would help his company to have a significant impact on one of the essential drivers of shareholder value and to maximize the utilization of their fixed assets.

PRODUCT LIFECYCLE MANAGEMENT AND THE NETWORKED SUPPLY CHAIN

New drugs come in all shapes and sizes. They also come with different levels of cost and service priorities. For example, a new type of aspirin would have a different service priority than a new heart drug.

In addition, new drugs often come with new manufacturing plant locations and new distribution channels. The ability to bring new drugs into an existing networked supply chain for both the new product introduction and the normal repeat volume is critical to the overall success of the drug and the pharmaceutical company. However, the ability to mainstream new drugs into existing manufacturing plants and supply

Exhibit 7-2. The five drivers of shareholder value.

Profitable Growth	Cost Minimization	Tax Minimization

| Working-Capital Efficiency | | Fixed-Capital Efficiency |

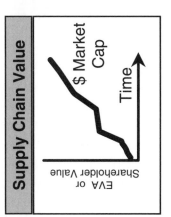

Supply Chain Value

$ Market Cap

Time

EVA or Shareholder Value

Return on Assets (PPE)
Network Optimization
Capacity Mgt/Throughput
Outsourcing

Source: Cap Gemini Ernst and Young.

chains enhances the leveraging of a pharmaceutical company's fixed assets, and, as such, their overall profitability.

PROFITABLE GROWTH THROUGH PLM—HOW TO GET STARTED

You read in this chapter about the challenges facing our CEO, Ted Crown. His largest challenge, and the largest challenge of an executive at any pharmaceutical company, is managing the development of new products in the pipeline. The implications of this process have significant impact on several drivers of shareholder value. Profitable growth is certainly heavily impacted. Because of patent expiration after seventeen years and the subsequent introduction of low-cost generic versions of the drug, the drug-development pipeline is the key to revenue growth in a pharmaceutical company. Additionally, the drug research and development process is a huge expense in this industry affecting two other drivers of shareholder value: cost minimization and fixed-capital minimization. Let us focus here on fixed-capital minimization and the steps necessary for minimizing this investment while maximizing the flow of new products into the pipeline. The key is effective management of the

---

Profitable Growth through PLM

Step 1:   Set the business strategy.

Step 2:   Manage knowledge.

Step 3:   Align people/organization.

Step 4:   Create effective business processes.

Step 5:   Develop an effective technology infrastructure.

product life cycle, which can be accomplished by attention to the following:

Step 1: Set the Business Strategy. In setting the business strategy, there must first be a clear understanding of the portfolio's risk profile. The probability of success at each stage of development must be assessed for each drug candidate. Then the aggregate portfolio risk profile can be understood. This understanding of the inherent risk in the portfolio is the first step in the development of an effective R&D strategy. It also helps to eliminate the surprise that Ted Crown experienced when his best drug candidate was unexpectedly eliminated.

After risks are assessed, criteria are established based upon the company's goals and priorities. For example, there may be a higher priority placed on specific therapeutic classes because of their market potential or other competitive situation. Once risks and criteria have been established, project priorities can be established, and low-value projects can be killed. For example, projects with low risk and high value based on the established criteria will be give highest priority, and projects with high risk and low value will be discontinued.

A process that clearly sets priorities and strategies will eliminate situations where more and more resources are sought so that all projects can be pursued instead of focusing on maximizing the throughput on the projects with the highest potential. This process helps to minimize fixed-asset requirements while, at the same time, expediting high-value drugs to market.

Step 2: Manage Knowledge. A pharmaceutical company's knowledge and content, that is, its intellectual capital, is the essential asset of the company. Therefore, this knowledge must be well-managed. An important concept is that of knowledge-sharing. Data must be centrally accessible throughout the company, and there must be a high degree of coordination. The objective is for everyone involved in R&D to collectively benefit from the knowledge and findings of each member of the research community. Sharing knowledge maximizes its value because it is reused in multiple situations, therefore reducing overall R&D expense. To effectively foster knowledge-sharing, there must be a high degree of accuracy and confidence in the data that is shared as well as rapid review and analysis of data.

With respect to managing the R&D portfolio, accurate up-to-date shared knowledge is essential to make effective, timely decisions. If knowledge is not effectively managed in that it is centrally accessible, it may take months to gather and analyze the data required to make decisions regarding the allocation of resources.

Step 3: Align People/Organization. People are the key to success in any organization. Therefore, it is essential that organizational structures and performance metrics be established so that everyone is working together to achieve the overall strategic goals of the company. There are multiple stakeholders in an organization, and the key is to ensure that all are working toward goals and performance objectives that are aligned with the corporate strategic goals. If priority has been given to certain drug candidates, then that priority should extend throughout the organization. Properly aligning performance objectives will help to mitigate in-fighting and power relationships, which compromise the quality of decisions.

Step 4: Create Effective Business Processes. The following items are important factors to consider when developing processes to manage a portfolio:

- The process must be driven by corporate strategy and goals.
- The process should be frequent and technology-enabled.
- The analysis must be factually based on real-time data.
- The emphasis must be on optimizing schedules and resources, not on cost and activity tracking.
- Capacity constraints must be understood and honored.
- Project plans must be easily adaptable in light of changing market and scientific data.

- Focus must be on the entire portfolio, not on a single project or user.
- The process must be clear and transparent to all stake-holders to ensure buy-in.

A process that includes these characteristics will ensure that the portfolio is managed such that resources are deployed to match corporate strategies and costs are minimized while throughput is maximized on the highest priority drug candidates.

Step 5: Develop an Effective Technology Infrastructure. To implement an effective product lifecycle management process, an effective technology infrastructure is required, which should include the following:

- A common consolidated tool throughout the company rather than a multitude of disconnected systems
- An emphasis on constraint-based planning so that schedules take into account available resources rather than scheduling beyond actual constraints and thereby creating infeasible schedules
- Optimization capabilities so that the portfolio and schedule have been developed to ensure that resources are used most effectively to meet corporate goals and objectives

The implementation of effective technology offers a key differentiator in the management of the R&D portfolio. Technology is essential if real-time decisions are to be made that optimize the utilization of resources.

Following the previous steps are the keys to reducing fixed-asset costs while maximizing revenue growth. In summary, the previous steps will provide you with the tools to:

- Maximize portfolio profitability.
- Accelerate high-margin projects.

- Rapidly terminate low-value projects.
- Respond faster to threats and opportunities.
- Increase development throughput.
- Streamline global R&D processes.

The result will be revenue growth, cost minimization, and an increase in shareholder value.

SUMMARY

After Paulina left, Ted sat back feeling much more comfortable than he had since that fateful day last week when he had first heard of the discontinuation of work on their most promising drug candidate. Perhaps this had been a much-needed wake-up call. He was confident that through their efforts to optimize the supply chain they could now efficiently manage their research and development portfolio.

The research and development process for pharmaceutical drug companies is the heart of their companies. It also dictates future investments in manufacturing plants and supply chain infrastructures. By instituting strong processes to professionally manage the new-product development process, pharmaceutical companies can increase both the number and percentage of successful new products. They will also enhance their connectivity to the networked supply chain by linking the new products into the existing supply chain infrastructure.

NOTES

1. PhRMA, Pharmaceutical Industry Profile 2000, Chapter 5, p.4.
2. Ibid., Chapter 3, pp. 41–42.
3. Ibid., Chapter 2, p. 1.

4. H. Grabowski, and Vernon, J., "Returns to R&D on New Drug Interactions in the 1980s," *Journal of Health Economics*, vol. 13, 1994.

5. *Windhover's Health Care Strategist*, 2000.

6. Elizabeth W. Boehm, with Eric G. Brown, Victoria M. Chiou, Sara E. Aurentz, and Stephanie Smith, "Sizing Healthcare eCommerce," *The Forrester Report*, December 1999.

8

THE CEO'S
AGENDA

INTRODUCTION

R ecently at a gathering of MBA students at a top business
school, we joined several students to discuss ways to
improve a company's wealth and operations in today's e-commerce global economy. Many of these top students had very
specific points of view, which was not surprising. What was
surprising was their functional views of how to improve a company's operations and the simplicity of their views on how to
create wealth within a company. Most of their points of view
centered first on reducing costs to drive profitability and second on top-line growth.

During our discussion, the subject of a CEO's agenda surfaced. The majority of the students again had very specific
points of view, which were centered on how CEOs could drive
top-line growth and reduce costs. It was obvious that there
were three main items that were not being considered by the
MBA students. These items were speed, the migration of a
company to a *.com*pany, and a vision for how the myriad of
electronic marketplaces in a blurred economy would fit together once they were built and operational.

SPEED

The Internet has had a significant impact on how we do business, how we behave as consumers, and how we recreate. It
has permeated even the smallest of life's challenges, from
changing a baby's diaper to the route we take to work everyday. The Internet offers immediate access to information and
the ability to make a transaction. In an earlier chapter, we
spoke of the airline pilot who used on-line information to update his flight plan in an on-line, real-time basis. It was a wonderful application of technology that produced positive cost

savings. However, what would happen if you were on the flight and the airline flight plan was not integrated with the air traffic controller or the ground crew at the destination? Would you think it was so wonderful to be either in a holding pattern for forty minutes or waiting on the ground until a gate became available? (How would you feel about waiting for your bags an extra forty minutes after a ten-hour flight because the flight plan was not linked with the labor scheduling of the baggage handlers?) An integrated and immediate response is now expected, and is permeating every action people take with the Internet.

During the holidays of 1999, several on-line retailers were unable to fill orders by Christmas. In fact, our neighbor's daughter received her Christmas toy on February 29, 2000. It was ordered in late November. Clearly, the brick-and-mortar supply chains have not kept pace with the Internet world's process of accepting orders. At least the toy was delivered before St. Patrick's Day!

THE CHALLENGES OF INTERNET SPEED

There are significant challenges that companies face when Internet-driven speed expectations are set. The following two questions highlight how difficult these challenges can be to overcome:

1. How fresh is the content connected to the Web sites?
2. How ready are the value-chain partners to respond to on-line virtual requests?

Content must have up-to-date information on products, pricing, promotions, and services to bridge the on-line requests to actual fulfillment capabilities. In the world of interoperability where customers want configured solutions, fresh content is virtually mandatory for customer satisfaction. Have you ever been on a Web site and struggled through old content? How many readers have experienced the thrill of the empty icon? People do not put up with empty icons for long, and tend not to return to the Web site once they have left. This represents lost market share and top-line growth for a company when it occurs. It would be better not to have a Web site at all than to have one with old content.

The integration of the value-chain partners (process and technology) is essential for the supply chain to respond to on-line virtual requests at Internet speed. The air traffic controller at the destination must be able to incorporate everyone's in-flight changes into their planning and scheduling of air traffic. The toy suppliers, manufacturers, transport providers, and third-party logistics companies must share access to on-line requests and have the processes to fulfill these requests in an expedited manner. If one participant in the supply chain is not properly integrated into the networked supply chain, then Christmas gifts can easily become Easter or spring break gifts. In networked supply chain management, the order-to-delivery process is only as fast as the slowest moving component. What we do know is that information cannot be the slowest moving component as it moves throughout the supply chain.

On a visit to a major retailer, the Internet order management department was observed printing on-line orders. These printed orders were then faxed to the store's order-entry department to be entered into the store's order-entry system. The store order-entry system was a proprietary, batch-driven system that had been custom-built. The information technology department had decided that it was too expensive to build a front-end system to electronically take orders from the company's own Web site! What resulted was a three-to-four-day time lag from the customer's placing an order over the Internet to the store's order-entry system accepting the order. In addition, the fulfillment of the order was through the traditional fulfillment process. This took another ten to fourteen days. The total elapsed time from the placement of the order to delivery was thirteen to eighteen days. Did we mention that the delivery was to the store, and not to the customer's house? We wondered whether the customer expected a *longer* delivery time by placing the order through the Web site! We also wondered why the retailer's brand and executive management teams had been left out of such a critical business decision made by the Information Technology department.

Let us go back to the CEO's agenda. The Internet has caused a speed expectation for orders placed on Web sites. This speed expectation has also carried over to traditional sales channels as well. The old brick-and-mortar supply chain fulfillment models are being challenged, and must be upgraded to click-and-brick models. The challenge is how a CEO can deconstruct a traditional supply chain fulfillment model and construct a click-and-brick model while maintaining existing business and meeting quarter-to-quarter expectations for Wall Street.

FROM COMPANY TO .COMPANY WEALTH

The majority of existing companies has time-tested products and supply chains. Sometimes, time-tested is a good thing. Frito Lay, Wal-Mart, and Toyota are solid examples of time-tested companies that have great products and services and superb supply chains. These companies have also been able to excel in growth, profit, and technology utilization. However, there are numerous examples of companies that have time-tested products but have not been able to concurrently excel at profit, growth, and technology utilization.

Sometimes, companies miss one essential item in their quest for excellence. Since the early 1980s, numerous companies have become proficient at reengineering their operations and driving profit by reducing costs. However, reducing costs does not directly correlate to driving growth. The companies that focus more on operating profit growth than revenue growth have been rewarded less by Wall Street than have their counterparts.

The Fortune 500 companies were compared to the industry averages in operating profit-growth rates and revenue-growth rates. These companies were then grouped into four quadrants based upon their performance with their industry peers. Not surprisingly, the slower operating profit/slower revenue-growth companies had the lowest aggregate market capital growth rate (77 percent), while the faster operating profit/faster revenue-growth companies had the highest aggregate market-capital growth rate (281 percent). What is surprising is that the slower operating profit/faster revenue-growth companies had a significantly higher aggregate market-capital growth rate (182 percent) than the faster operating profit/slower revenue-growth companies (131 percent), as depicted in Exhibit 8-1. Clearly, Wall Street is rewarding growth and profits before it rewards growth over profit.

However, profit and growth are not the only games in Wall Street anymore for driving shareholder value. Technology utilization and intangibles have ascended to equal positions of importance in today's global economy, as illustrated in Exhibit 8-2. To be truly rewarded by Wall Street, a company must excel at all four. The goal must be to achieve a score of at least eight, on a scale of one to ten, in each category.

Driving operating profits in today's e-business world is significantly more difficult than it was in the past. Companies need reliable and efficient Web-enabled networked supply chains to meet customers' expectations of the Internet (or be faced with providing Christmas toys at Easter). Companies need to consider sharing services like e-exchanges, outsourcing noncore functions, and developing timely and accurate reporting systems. All of these capabilities need to be built around speed.

Revenue growth has to start with the customer. Right now, regardless of industry, the battle in the marketplace is for

Exhibit 8-1. Growth eclipsing profit in driving shareholder value today. . . . .

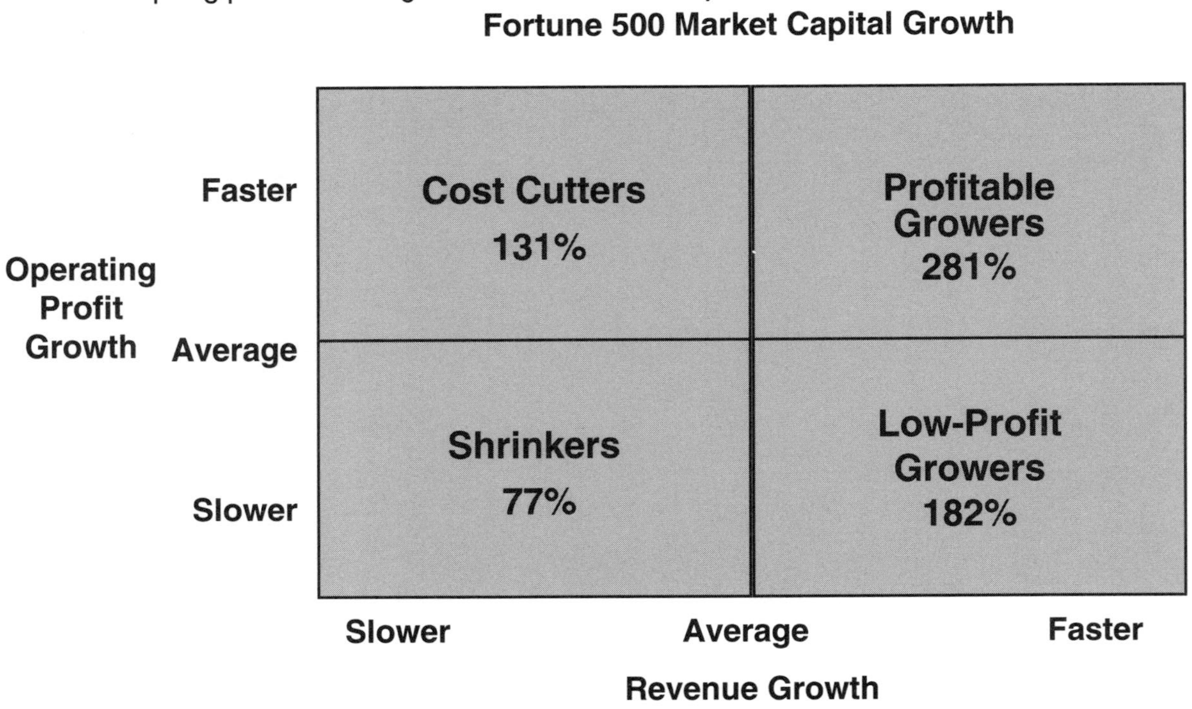

Fortune 500 Market Capital Growth

		Revenue Growth	
Operating Profit Growth		Slower / Average	Faster
Faster / Average		Cost Cutters 131%	Profitable Growers 281%
Slower		Shrinkers 77%	Low-Profit Growers 182%

Source: Cap Gemini Ernst & Young.

Exhibit 8-2. Technology utilization and intangibles ascending to equal positions of importance in driving *.company*™ wealth.

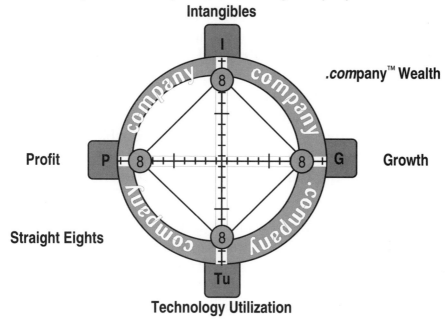

Source: Cap Gemini Ernst & Young.

control of the customers' wallets. Loyalty is earned, not reengineered. Customer insights help to develop strong customer relationships with proven brands. In the Internet world, strong customer relationships are developed around customer solutions. The home office and all of its contents represent one customer solution. Another may be the garage, and still another might be the kitchen. People put all the items together in a home office. The winner of tomorrow will be the one to configure all the components in a home office, schedule the components for delivery, and assemble the components at one time. This includes telephones, telephone lines, desktop computers, printers, fax machines, office desks, chairs, filing cabinets, and even the pictures on the wall. Configuration is a key, but fulfillment of the solution is the differentiator.

Technology utilization has climbed the corporate ladder faster than the market caps of many *com*panies. As recently as five to ten years ago, it was almost unheard of for CEOs to discuss technology utilization. Today, if it is not the first thing that they talk about with security analysts, it is the second or third item. Connectivity to customers and actual customer demand are essential in today's world of free and instant information access. The linkage of suppliers to this on-line customer demand is also critical for speed in the supply chain to quickly satisfy customer demand. This linkage can be self-service or it can be interactive. Whatever it is, it must enable the development of customer and supplier relationships and build on the momentum of the brand's image and presence in the marketplace.

However, what about all of those companies that are Internet start-ups with little or no revenue, no profits, and market caps in the billions? These are truly times of insanity. What is Wall Street looking for in these companies? If we knew exactly, we would not be writing this book. We would be in the Bahamas on-line with E*Trade at $8 per trade and enjoying the sun and surf. However, on the serious side, we have locked in on one thing that analysts do look for in companies trying to bring their companies into the Internet age. They are looking for intangibles, or in other words, "net future expectations."

Companies must have a credible e-commerce strategy. This includes a business-to-business and a business-to-consumer strategy. They must also have an aggressive implementation plan that includes a detailed outline of how to prove the effectiveness of their plan. To accomplish these objectives, companies must blend in-house development, alliances with third-party experts, and strategic acquisitions. Much as our CEO did with the help of a war room in Chapter 1, executives must use a strong public relations effort to tell Wall Street and the marketplace about their companies' e-commerce plans and e-fulfillment accomplishments.

Again, let us revisit the CEO's agenda. The CEO must fulfill all four objectives—driving operating profits, revenue growth, technology utilization, and intangibles—and hopefully score an eight to create lasting shareholder value or *.com*pany wealth. If you had to rate your company on each of the four categories, how would your company score? Use your own industry average as a four, and measure your company from one to ten using the *.com*pany wealth chart, as depicted in Exhibit 8-3.

FROM COMPANY TO *.COMPANY* OPERATIONS

To be a *.com*pany is to be scalable in execution. Companies have to move from being variable to stable to scalable to succeed in today's Internet-driven world, as illustrated in Exhibit 8-4. Most manufacturers are stable. This means that they can execute to volumes that approximate their production capacity, plus or minus 10 to 15 percent. Scalable means a company can handle a 50 percent swing in demand overnight. Toyota is trying to move its capital-intensive business from stable to scalable with its five-day order-to-ship program. It takes these types of breakthroughs in execution to achieve scalability in the Internet economy.

Exhibit 8-3. *.company*™ wealth: How do you rate?

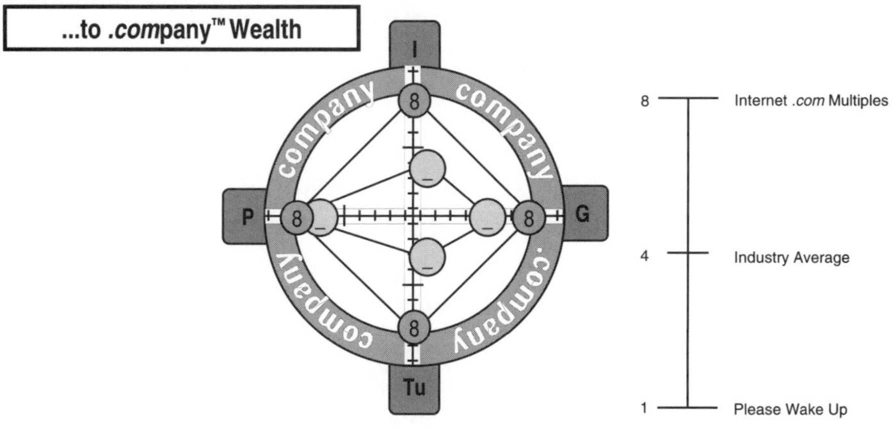

Source: Cap Gemini Ernst & Young.

Exhibit 8-4. From company to .company™ operations.

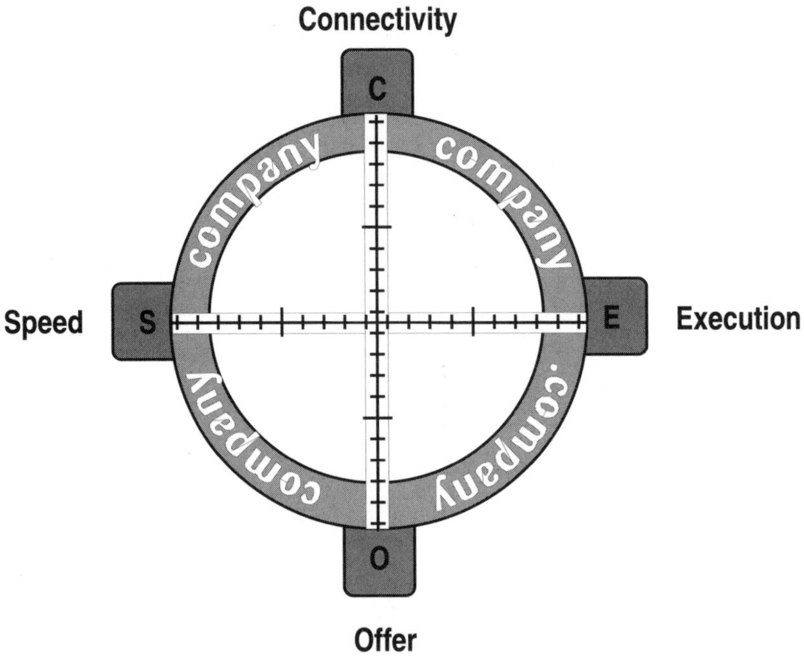

Connectivity

Speed ... **Execution**

Offer

Source: Cap Gemini Ernst & Young.

Connectivity means more than connecting two dots. It means migrating from interfacing with other functions within the enterprise to interfacing with other companies in the value chain to interoperability. We discussed the in-flight changes in a flight plan on an international flight. To connect with all affected parties on an on-line, real-time basis and to adjust their operations accordingly is achieving excellence in connectivity.

The offer to customers needs to connect to customer values. It is not just about placing a commodity for the best bid. The appropriate solution provider should track a customer who uses an Internet solution provider to build his or her home office. Periodic offers should be extended as the customer relationship grows stronger. For example, a change in jobs may mean an upgrade to an ISDN line, a faster printer, and an upgrade in a cellular telephone. Bundling these options together in an upgrade offer will provide immense value to the customer if it is done on a timely basis.

As mentioned earlier, the movement from a company to a .*com*pany is about speed. This means speed in making the offer to the customer, speed in taking the customer's order, speed in connecting and communicating to networked supply chain partners, speed in executing, and speed in delivery. It means speed in a company's responsiveness to customer demand. This also means that all of the old organizational paradigms have to shift to one of speed.

Again, rate your company on each scale to determine where on the .*com*pany operations scale your company resides. Be realistic, because your competitors are moving at Internet speed, as depicted in Exhibit 8-5.

How do technology utilization, intangibles, and e-exchanges fit together? To the average person, much less the CEO of a major Global 1000 company, there appears to be a rush for everyone to build his or her own e-exchanges and pri-

Exhibit 8-5. .*company*™ wealth: How do you rate?

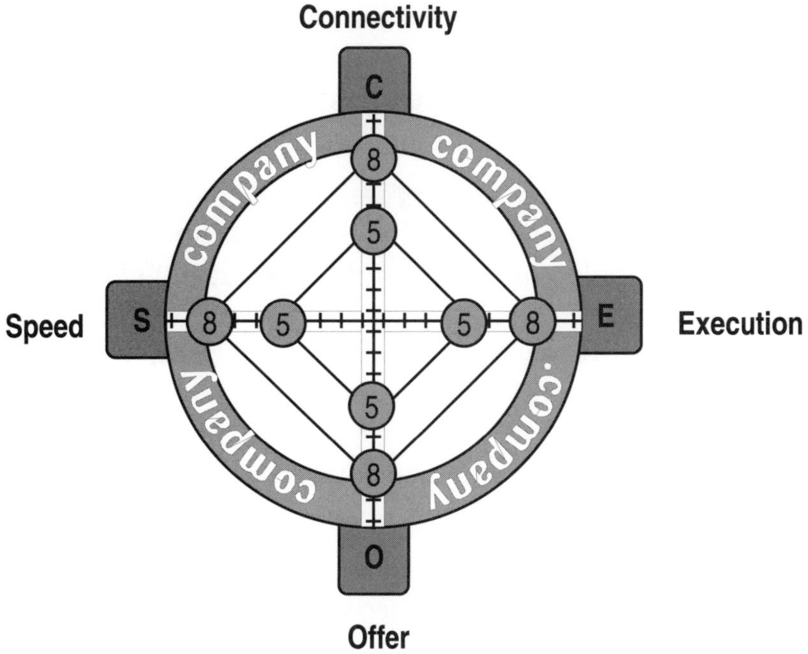

Source: Cap Gemini Ernst & Young.

vate networks. Somehow, they must all be linked, or suppliers and customers will forever be confused. In addition, the cost savings from using technology will be evaporated by the need to work with multiple, stand-alone exchanges. We discussed briefly in Chapter 3 that the other benefit of HightechMatrix was its ability to link to other trade marketplaces. Let us take a look at how this is possible.

TRADEMATRIX™

Throughout the book, there are specific examples of trading or e-exchanges in various industries. These trading exchanges are usually focused on a specific industry, with two or three large trading partners anchoring the exchange. Each solution appears to be independent of the other, providing no leveraging of information from one source to another. Each solution has its own technological architecture and standards. Many of the existing exchanges are transaction-oriented, supporting only spot-buying and selling. Customer solutions that cross industry boundaries are left out of the equation. In addition, as we mentioned in an earlier chapter, customer-facing solutions are frequently not linked to fulfillment processes.

In the future, purchasing professionals will demand intelligent procurement processes that span multiple trading sites and portals. Suppliers will demand the ability to electronically present their goods and services, and those of their trading partners, to purchasing professionals. In addition, new product development designers will demand on-line, 24×7 design and development collaboration to optimally allocate scarce resources to the prioritized new products in their pipelines.

The next generation of trading exchanges will encompass decision support processes (decision-flows) that evaluate multiple courses of action before arriving at an optimal solution and committing to a specific course of action. For example, the real-time order management capability in the networked supply chain uses decision-flows to determine configuration capability and price before an order is accepted. Multiply this scenario millions of times with countless participants, and the potential and the complexity increases exponentially.

E-commerce buyers and sellers are demanding access to worldwide Web sites through a single portal entry. However, they want access to all other portals and exchange marketplaces. This one-to-many outlook holds an enormous potential for both buyers and sellers.

Throughout the chapters, there was also a focus on process excellence. From the customer focus in Chapter 2 to networked supply chain excellence in Chapter 3 to product lifecycle management in Chapter 7, companies are relying on supporting technologies as they execute commerce over the Web. Without these supporting technologies, networked supply chain process excellence at Internet speed cannot be achieved.

TradeMatrix™ is an intelligent business portal that spans multiple digital marketplaces, as depicted in Exhibit 8-6. It uses advanced optimization and execution capabilities to improve decision making across multiple digital marketplaces. It manages diverse workflows as well as market mechanisms, such as auctioning. It also combines services for buyers, sellers, designers, and service providers to optimize the buying and selling processes. It also uses speed to uncover missed value that other time-constrained methods may miss.

As companies transform themselves to .companies, they need to address all the issues mentioned previously. TradeMatrix supports the .company transformation through procurement, commerce, fulfillment, planning, customer care, and new product development services.

TradeMatrix™ and the .Company

The procurement services of a .company include basic purchasing activities such as product specifications, request for

Exhibit 8-6. TradeMatrix.™

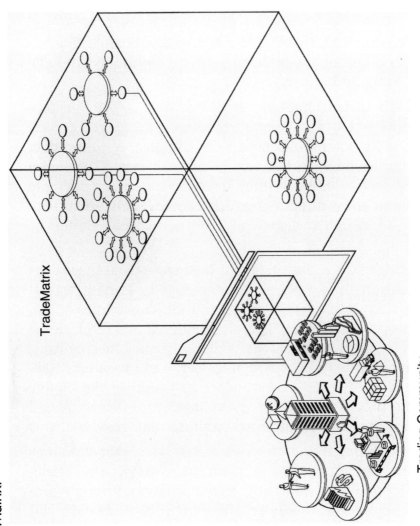

TradeMatrix

Trading Community

Source: i2 Technologies.

bids, and auctions. These services include direct and indirect materials, and center around the consolidation of purchases to reduce purchasing costs. Included in these services is connectivity to supply chain partners through multiple digital marketplaces to help ensure execution of the customer's order. This execution includes the assurance of availability and on-time delivery of the customer's ordered items.

The commerce services include services such as brand management and product portfolio positioning. The key in these services is the exposure of a product portfolio to multiple exchanges or Web sites. For example, if a major company wanted to sell 1,000 PCs as part of its technology upgrade plan, it could have its offer to sell 1,000 PCs on multiple digital marketplaces through TradeMatrix. As such, the reach or exposure to new customers and channels and the speed of this expanded exposure are greatly enhanced.

The fulfillment services involve linking on-line buyers and sellers (procurement and commerce) to essential supply chain fulfillment partners. These partners can range from transportation and warehousing companies to .comLLPs, such as Ryder Logistics. The connectivity between supply chain partners to perform the necessary planning activities is crucial for superior execution.

The product development services provide a planning hub for new product development projects, market feedback, and customer collaboration. The insights gained from this customer collaboration accelerate the speed at which new product development can produce winning products into the marketplace. Revenue growth and subsequent operating profit result from these services.

Planning services incorporate the complexities of multiple supply chain partners to solve complex demand-fulfillment requests. By using supply chain constraints such as the availability of raw materials and finished products, expected customer service levels, perfect order fill expectations, cost, and the availability of transportation and warehousing services, the best fulfillment solutions can be secured through the Internet in a matter of hours, not days or weeks.

Customer care services focus on ensuring that the customer is satisfied after the sale. These services can be linked to other customer care centers that focus on customer satisfaction throughout the life cycle of the products acquired.

The TradeMatrix solution to the multiple digital marketplaces or exchanges maps well to the primary drivers of companies transitioning to *.com*pany operations. Throughout the multiple services of TradeMatrix, speed, execution, offer, and connectivity are prevalent and prominent.

THE CEO'S AGENDA— HOW TO GET STARTED

To operate a CEO's agenda, an executive must adopt the frameworks of wealth and operations. These frameworks allow the executive to assess the current state, visualize the future

---

The CEO's Agenda

Step 1: Assess your company's current state in *.com*pany wealth.

Step 2: Assess your company's current state in *.com*pany operations.

Step 3: Review strategies for achieving "straight eights" in both *.com*pany wealth and *.com*pany operations.

Step 4: Identify skill sets needed by executives to operate in a *.com*pany.

Step 5: Select the right technology partner(s) for the transformed *.com*pany.

Step 6: Implement the *.com*pany strategies.

state, and determine what areas to pursue on a priority basis. The critical success factor here is to pursue the priority areas at Internet speed. The following steps will help the executive to get started on achieving "straight eights" in the Internet-enabled world:

Step 1: Assess your company's current state in .company wealth. As stated earlier, the transformation from company to .company wealth involves operating profits, revenue growth, technology utilization, and intangibles. In this step, you should review your earlier assessment of your company and how it is performing in your industry. The industry average is a score of four for each category. The more advanced companies will have suppliers, vendors, and customers that rate your company as well. Remember that the critical success factor in this step is honesty. Improvement cannot start without the accurate and honest assessment of the current state.

Step 2: Assess your company's current state in .company operations. The transformation from company to .company operations involves connectivity, scalability, speed, and the offer. In this step, as in Step 1, you should review the assessment you made earlier in the chapter about your company and how it is performing in your industry. Again, the industry average is a score of four for each category. In the networked supply chain, suppliers and customers can have even more impact through involvement in this assessment.

Step 3: Review strategies for achieving "straight eights" in both .company wealth and operations. The objective is to achieve at least a score of eight in all categories. Once the assessments in Steps 1 and 2 are completed, a simple gap analysis should be performed for each category. After the gap analysis, the categories with the greatest performance gaps should be prioritized. Our recommendation is to pick one category in .company wealth and one category in .company operations on which to focus the company's transformation efforts. Nothing sells like success. The demonstrated ability to move the line between these two categories will have a positive effect on the company's ability to support future efforts in the other six categories. Of course, we are not advocating that the company ignores the other six categories. We are advocating a balanced approach for the other six, while a disproportionate amount of executive focus is placed on the two highest opportunity categories.

Step 4: Identify the skillsets needed by executives to operate in a .com*pany.* The ability of an executive to operate in a .company is highly dependent on the development of new skill sets. Four different skill sets are needed by the .company executive as shown in Exhibit 8-7. Using a scale that has .company intensity on the Y-axis and networked supply chain complexity on the X-axis, the four primary skill sets are defined. The primary skill set involving low .company intensity and low networked supply chain complexity is execution. The objective in this quadrant is to win through the achievement of functional efficiencies. The primary skill set involving low .company intensity and high networked supply chain complexity is partnering. The objective of this quadrant is to achieve a win/win situation with networked supply chain partners to achieve process effectiveness. The primary skill set involving high .company intensity and low networked supply chain complexity is negotiation. The objective of this quadrant is to achieve a win/win situation with selected networked supply chain partners or noncompeting but similar companies to achieve throughput velocity with infrastructure leverage. The last quadrant is perhaps the differentiator for an executive to achieve personal transformation from company to .company. The primary skill set involving high .company intensity and high networked supply chain complexity is collaboration. The objective of this quadrant is to achieve a win/win/win situation with all involved (suppliers, customers, venture capitalists, and alliance partners) to achieve innovation around net future expectations. The strategy around collaboration is to know when to create alliances and when to decouple from alliances, such as market opportunities and technological change. The essen-

Exhibit 8-7. Future .company™ skills needed for the networked supply chain.

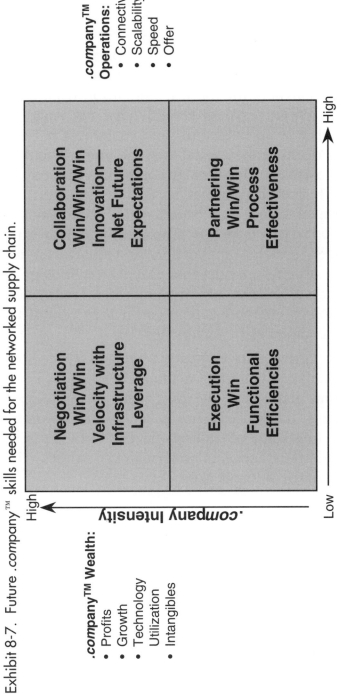

.company™ Wealth:
- Profits
- Growth
- Technology Utilization
- Intangibles

.company™ Intensity

High

Negotiation
Win/Win
Velocity with
Infrastructure
Leverage

Collaboration
Win/Win/Win
Innovation—
Net Future
Expectations

Execution
Win
Functional
Efficiencies

Partnering
Win/Win
Process
Effectiveness

Low

Networked Supply Chain Complexity

High

.company™ Operations:
- Connectivity
- Scalability
- Speed
- Offer

tial message in this quadrant is to create through innovation and avoid producing through total control. This is very different and challenging to most senior executives who have earned their success by producing with total control.

Step 5: Select the right technology partner(s) for the transformed .company. One critical item is to select the correct technology partners for the transformation from company to .company. These partners should have not only a demonstrated ability to add value to their customers but a vision of what opportunities are available in the immediate future. Our advice is to look for technology companies that have successfully transformed themselves as technology and the marketplace have changed. For example, i2 Technologies quickly transformed itself from an advanced planning and scheduling (APS) systems application provider to an intelligent e-business systems provider that provides technology-based solutions such as HightechMatrix.com and TradeMatrix. How can technology companies help you if they cannot transform their own companies to .companies?

Step 6: Implement .company strategies. Once Steps 1 to 5 are complete, implementation should begin. This is a journey, and in some industries, the road maps are redesigned every month. Thus, the process should be an iterative one. This includes the upgrading of skill sets needed to thrive in the .company. In addition, action is preferred over studies. Time waits for no one in the Internet age.

SUMMARY

The CEO's agenda is changing drastically in today's e-commerce global economy. To improve its wealth and operations, the CEO must transition his or her company from a company to a .company. To improve wealth, the company must outperform its competition in profit, revenue generation, technology utilization, and intangibles. To improve operations, the company must outperform its competition in connectivity, offer, scalability, and speed. Merely outperforming the competition is no longer good enough. To be a *.company*, you must score an eight in all eight measures.

Speed and technology utilization must be pervasive in the future success of any networked supply chain. E-commerce solutions such as TradeMatrix must exist to achieve speed. The CEO must rethink how business is currently performed, and create both the vision and sense of urgency for change. Perhaps the same MBA students can return to their campus after a year in the e-commerce world and tell younger students what should be on a CEO's agenda. We are positive that the answers would be dramatically different from the ones that surfaced during our discussions. If you were a CEO for a day, what would be on your agenda?

9

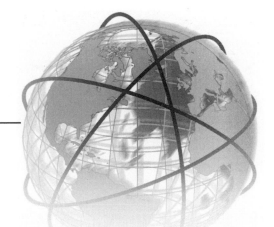

THE NEXT WAVE

OF SUPPLY

CHAIN VALUE

CHANGE? WHAT CHANGE?

In mid-March 2000, there was an announcement that several consumer products companies had agreed to be part of a large global industry-wide Internet marketplace. The announcement stated that this assembly of consumer products manufacturers was accomplished during a two-week period. It also stated that the goal was to achieve supply chain efficiencies, and that details about the new company's structure and equity stakes were to be worked out at a later date.[1]

Privately, a senior executive from one of the involved consumer products companies stated that the purpose of this announcement was to let Wall Street know that they were going to do something that had an "e" in front of it. He stated that there was no intention of doing anything different using the Internet marketplace except for the procurement of noncritical commodities. In fact, he stated that his company would lose competitive positioning in the marketplace if it allowed a "committee of his peers" to dictate how his company should manage its critical purchasing and supply chain activities.

Within days of this announcement, the on-line grocer Peapod, Inc., announced that its ability to keep operating was questionable after losing its chief executive and a cash infusion. The announcement had implications that extended beyond Peapod to other profitless e-commerce companies that depend on the promise of net future expectations.[2] Barry Stouffer, a senior analyst covering Internet grocers at J.C. Bradford & Co. of Nashville, Tennessee, stated, "It is symptomatic of the New Economy where companies are able to go public with unproven business models when they are still losing money."[3] Peapod never earned a penny, and its market capitalization plummeted. Peapod was eventually purchased by Ahold, a very large European-based grocery chain.

There are three lessons to be learned from these unrelated announcements. The first lesson is that CEOs are being hammered by Wall Street to do something with an "e" in front of it. The second lesson (which pertains more to the first announcement) is that a public Internet marketplace with a management committee made up of competitive peers will reduce the value of the exchange to only noncritical commodity items, such as cleaning solvents and travel. The third lesson is the hardest. It involves commitment to true leadership and change by using a strong business plan. The CEO who commented on his participation in the Internet marketplace had virtually no commitment to true and lasting change. He was not embracing the concept of transformation from a company to a *.com*pany, nor did he have the interest to do so. Peapod had a vision and was forging new ground in growing its customer base. However, many questioned the profitability of its ongoing business case. As the five drivers of shareholder value show, lasting shareholder value can only be achieved by concurrently attaining cost minimization, tax minimization, working-capital efficiency, fixed-capital efficiency, and profitable growth. If a company significantly misses one driver, as Peapod did, and lose profitable growth, Wall Street will make it pay dearly!

THERE IS SPEED, AND THERE IS STUPIDITY

Our CEO in Chapter 1 needed to respond to security analysts *with substance* after a fire disrupted his manufacturing capacity and his ability to serve customers. The use of collaboration and technology enabled him to restructure his supply chain and introduce an e-commerce strategy within his company. The use of Web-based catalogues and scan-based trading is helping to drive supply chain efficiencies in the retail consumer products industries. Networked supply chains with demand and supply communicators, such as HightechMatrix.com, are transforming the lightning-quick world of PC manufacturing. Even slow-moving industries, such as oil and gas, pharmaceuticals, and transportation, are experiencing transformation by using Internet-based technologies.

The critical success factor is to transform a company to a *.company* with a balanced focus on driving wealth and improving operations. Transformation is more than a group press release with an "e" in front of it. Transformation involves understanding the industry and company dynamics, and then incorporating e-based processes and technologies to connect the extended supply chain network to the end customers.

These same security analysts will be waiting for CEOs of major companies to update the Wall Street community about their progress in transforming their companies to *.com*panies. They will also be demanding results! They will demand that the CEO have a vision, strategy, and a transformation business plan, plus the ability to move the company swiftly toward his or her vision.

What should be on a CEO's agenda, and how should a CEO plan to communicate to security analysts in the topsy-turvy world of the Internet? The scenarios in this book were designed to help CEOs understand the dynamics of each industry, and to provide technology-enabled solutions for their transformation efforts. The CEO who explains his or her e-commerce strategy in terms of an industry-wide Internet marketplace that is run by executives from his or her competitors will have a lot of questions to answer from his or her shareholders.

THE SUPPLY CHAIN NETWORK IN THE INTERNET WORLD

The concept of supply chain management has blurred into the basic activity of matching supply with consumer demand. The use of the Internet to capture actual customer demand has sped past most companies' abilities to fulfill the demand at Internet speed. A networked supply chain is not something that can be created overnight, or even in two weeks! It requires a holistic transformation process that is customer-focused, technology-enabled, and process-driven. People must embrace the transformation, from suppliers to manufacturers to retailers or dealers to customers. All participants in the networked supply chain must collaborate and be Web-connected to achieve networked supply chain excellence at Internet speed.

THE DEAN OF INFORMATION-TECHNOLOGY SUPPLY CHAIN MANAGEMENT

There was one man who had a vision of a technology-enabled networked supply chain built on collaboration. His name was Ken Sharma (see photo below).[4]

Sharma was vice chairman and senior partner of i2 Technologies from 1988 until his death in 1999. His impact on the development of supply chain planning—and the future of e-business—continues to resonate today.

The son of a diplomat in the Indian foreign service, Sharma was born in Burma in 1940 and grew up in the United Kingdom. After earning a bachelor of arts in electrical engineering from India's Benares Hindu University, he went on to attend graduate school at Cornell University, where he studied operations research.

During the 1980s, Sharma worked for Creative Output, a scheduling software company. While working at Creative Output, Sharma began a partnership with Dr. Eli Goldratt, the acclaimed author of *The Goal*, and began to develop concepts using a methodology known as the theory of constraints. Sharma also spent fifteen years in material and manufacturing systems for Texas Instruments, eventually becoming vice president of operations.

In 1988, Sanjiv Sidhu, founder of the technology start-up Intellection, recognized that Sharma could apply his knowledge of multiple constraint management to problems arising from supply chain planning. Sidhu offered him 18 percent of his fledgling company if Sharma would join as cofounder. The two men were also drawn together by their common beliefs—both dreamed of running a company where work was ethical, customer service was a top priority, and individual ego was unimportant.

Rejecting traditional resource management and cost-accounting methods, Sharma hit on the breakthrough technology for i2—an advanced algorithm for supply chain planning. From this initial work grew the constraint-based design that underlies i2's RHYTHM™ software, and i2's entire solution set for today's e-business.

By 1996, Sharma and Sidhu had been jointly named Ernst & Young's high-tech entrepreneur of the year for the

Southwest region, and their company, now i2 Technologies, had become the first supply chain management company to earn $100 million in revenue. In 1998, RHYTHM won *Industry Week's* "Technology of the Year" award, and i2 promised to return $50 billion in value to its customers by 2005. The recent i2 merger with Aspect Development became the largest in the history of the software industry.

Throughout his career, Sharma worked to define and refine the concepts of global optimization, multi-enterprise planning, master planning, and supply chain planning. His leadership and vision helped not only to make i2 the top provider of intelligent e-business solutions but also to change the paradigms by which industries understand concepts such as supply chain planning and technology. Most important, even as Sharma changed the face of business, he never flagged in his dedication to what he did. As he once said, "This work of mine has been a great source of satisfaction . . . If I've been able to help at least one person, that will be enduring."

Ken Sharma would be proud of the way supply chain management has evolved into networked supply chain management. His work and dedication to the industry helped to make this transformation a reality. He certainly deserves the title of the dean of IT supply chain management.

CONCLUSION

Technology is driving companies to become .companies in timeframes that are testing even the very best senior executives in the best companies. Wall Street expectations have never been higher. Neither have the expectations of customers, suppliers, and employees. The pressure to transform companies at Internet speed is intense, to say the least.

The era of the next generation of supply chain management is upon us. Technology-enabled solutions are at the heart of the transformation process for companies to become .companies. They are also at the heart of customer satisfaction with Internet speed. Customer satisfaction can only be achieved through an order configuration and fulfillment process that supports actual customer demand.

Who will be the next dean of the networked supply chain? The marketplace is waiting. In the meantime, the era of the networked supply chain has begun!

Notes

1. Shelly Branch, "Over 50 Consumer Products Concerns To Forge Industry Web Marketplace," *The Wall Street Journal*, March 16, 2000, p. B18.
2. Bill Spurgeon and Jim Carlton, "Peapod Weighs Sale, Options After Two Setbacks," *The Wall Street Journal*, March 17, 2000, p. A3.
3. Ibid.
4. Kate Luce, "Ken Sharma," *Skutski & Oltmanns* for i2 Technologies, March 17, 2000, pp. 1–2.

Appendix A

TRADING
COMMUNITIES
AND THEIR
IMPORTANCE
IN THE
NETWORKED
SUPPLY CHAIN

TRADING COMMUNITIES

A "trading community" is the coming together of buyers and sellers around a specific focal point. Trading communities can develop around types of commodities or products being traded. These trading communities evolve around a "horizontal portal." Trading communities can also evolve around specific industries. These trading communities evolve around a "vertical portal." Some trading communities come together, and intersect specific commodities or products (horizontal portals) with specific industries (vertical portals.) These trading communities evolve around an "integrated network," or a multiple of horizontal and vertical portal operators.

Public trading communities are trading communities that are open to any buyer and seller. Usually these communities are focused on auction sites that bring buyers and sellers together. E-Bay is an example of a public trading community.

Private trading communities are trading communities with specific trading partners. These trading partners have specific agreements in place that monitor the transaction services between the partners. These agreements govern the flow of goods, information, and financial transactions. The private trading partners work together on a private network, and must have a series of passcodes to enter through the multiple firewalls on the network. AutoLink and Covisint are examples of private trading communities.

HORIZONTAL PORTALS

Horizontal portals (Exhibit A-1) are established to have many buying organizations gain access to many suppliers. A horizontal portal can be "many-to-many" or "one-to-many." The in-

Exhibit A-1. Trading communities: horizontal portals.

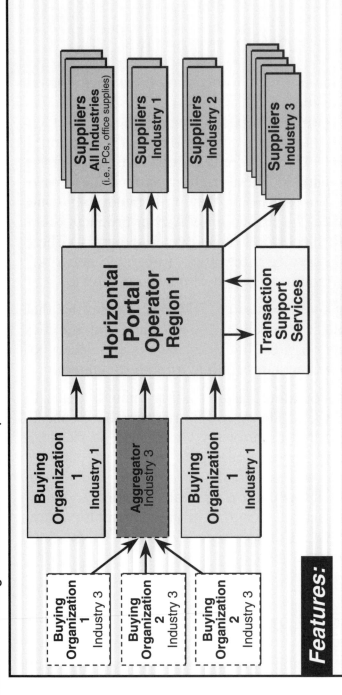

Features:

● Buying organizations in any industry can access any suppliers on the portal.

● Excellent access to suppliers of indirect goods regardless of industry specific needs (PCs, photocopiers, paper).

● A buying organization can set up an industry "aggregator site" (i.e., industry vertical portal) to consolidate purchases of a particular industry.

● Portal may provide other services to buying organizations and sellers such as customs, freight, insurance, cash settlement, credit monitoring, auctions, etc.

Source: Cap Gemini Ernst & Young.

dustry is not a driving force behind the development of a horizontal portal. These portals usually involve materials that are not directly involved in the main production or assembly of goods. The driving forces behind a horizontal portal are cost-reduction and standardization.

Many trading communities have been formed around horizontal portals. The focus of these portals is primarily on indirect materials. These materials range from office products such as paper, photocopiers, and personal computers to factory products such as cleaning solvents and paper towels. These horizontal portals represent the easiest point of entry into e-procurement because they involve materials that do not provide a competitive advantage to any one particular buyer.

In many cases, the administrative cost to acquire indirect materials can be greater than the cost of the materials themselves. In a recent internal study conducted by Cap Gemini Ernst & Young US for a major industry group, the average total cost of an indirect material order was $137.50. The product cost was $71.00, while the administrative cost to place and receive the order was $66.50! These costs did not include inventory-carrying costs, estimated to be high within the confines of the total cost of the indirect material order. Every diffused order point for office products and factory cleaning products had their own safety stock inventory. Due to the lack of electronic ordering and inventory receipt of the indirect materials, a company-wide physical count of these indirect materials was extremely difficult and almost impossible to do accurately.

The above example included many diverse ordering points for indirect materials, many local and a few national suppliers, and frequently a manual process for the order person to aggregate the demand, and place the indirect material orders. Orders were placed by telephone to the supplier. Invoices were reconciled by what deal the local ordering point had with their direct supplier contact. In many cases, local outlets for national companies had a multitude of "deal sheets" that did not match the pricing schedules in the national agreements between the two companies.

Because the cost of these products is relatively low, the study found that the time spent on searching for information and overall transaction administration was relatively high. In several cases, the ordering personnel used suppliers that were not authorized due to convenience. This activity contributes to a dilution of purchasing volumes that provide the basis for national price/volume schedules within annual agreements. Overall, the entire network pays a higher price for the convenience choice of local ordering personnel.

In the networked supply chain, horizontal portals can provide other services besides the procurement of indirect materials. These services include customs clearance, transportation load-matching, insurance, cash settlement, international shipping document administration, and credit monitoring.

Another service of a horizontal portal is a reverse logistics auction site. These auction sites provide an electronic meeting place for suppliers to place their excess goods and receive bids from multiple buyers. Examples of these goods are merchandise left over from a particular sale on a retailer's trade calendar, cancelled orders, or seasonal goods (e.g., lawn chairs and swimsuits) not sold by the end of the selling season.

The value of horizontal portals is in cost reduction and simplification of complexity. It involves connecting many buyers to many suppliers across a multitude of industries, while enabling one buyer to connect to many suppliers or one supplier to many buyers.

VERTICAL PORTALS

Vertical portals (Exhibit A-2) enable business services provided by the vertical portal to buyers and suppliers within a vertical or industry sector. Covisint AutoLink are two ex-

Exhibit A-2. Trading communities: vertical portals.

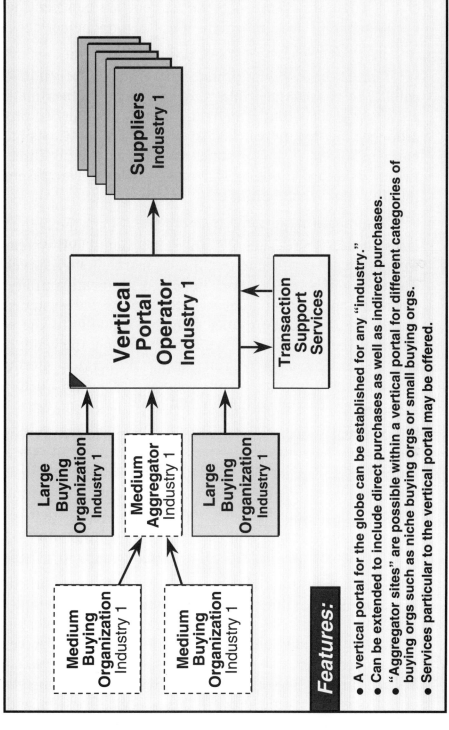

Features:

- A vertical portal for the globe can be established for any "industry."
- Can be extended to include direct purchases as well as indirect purchases.
- "Aggregator sites" are possible within a vertical portal for different categories of buying orgs such as niche buying orgs or small buying orgs.
- Services particular to the vertical portal may be offered.

Source: Cap Gemini Ernst & Young.

changes that are examples of vertical portals. Neither Covisint nor AutoLink have immediate plans to provide services outside the automotive industry sector.

One of the key differentiators of a vertical portal is its capability to be extended into direct materials. Direct materials are any materials that are directly part of the finished product produced by the networked supply chain. In Covisint, the parts, sub-systems, and systems supplied by the tier three, tier two, and tier one suppliers all come together and are assembled into the final vehicle product.

Another differentiator of a vertical portal is the type of services offered. The design of parts, sub-systems, and systems for a new vehicle is critical to the time-to-market for a new vehicle. The ability of a vertical portal operator to create a utility that suppliers can share and collaborate on parts, sub-systems, and systems designs can produce immense benefits to the entire automotive networked value chain. Remember the water pump example in Chapter 4? A vertical portal operator offering design collaboration services on a global basis would help solve this problem for the automotive OEM in question.

Vertical portals are also emerging in niche areas within an industry sector or vertical. There are vertical portals springing up in tier three, tier two, and tier one supplier communities that function as "aggregator sites." These vertical portals are designed to provide industry-specific services to their respective community of companies while offering the connectivity to other industry portals.

We discussed in "Horizontal Portals" the networked supply chain services of customs clearance, transportation load-matching, insurance, cash settlement, international shipping document administration, and credit monitoring. A vertical portal operator can also provide these same services to suppliers and buyers. The only difference would be that the vertical portal operator would provide these services customized to a specific industry sector. This can have a distinct advantage to a vertical portal customer. For example, the shipper of automotive engines can have specific customs clearance and shipment documentation. It can also have access to shipment testing services that provide value-add packaging recommendations for ocean shipping conditions.

If we take the automotive vertical portal one step further, other services can be aggregated and provided to vertical portal customers. These services are warranty information storage, maintenance catalogs, part and sub-system history and interchangeability, tracking part and service performance, virtual inventory pooling, integration with logistics providers, and regulatory interfaces.

INTEGRATED NETWORK

An integrated network (Exhibit A-3) involves trading communities coming together, and intersects specific commodities or products (horizontal portals) with specific industries (vertical portals.) The entire network of suppliers is shared with the entire network of buyers.

A good example of an emerging integrated network is Fasturn. Fasturn is a global business-to-business marketplace providing portal services to the apparel industry. Dr. Frank Litvack founded it in February 1999.

Fasturn started by offering horizontal portal services to garment suppliers, agents, and buyers worldwide. An example of Fasturn's horizontal portal offering is their auction site. Sellers can place their goods on the auction site with either a predetermined price or a dynamic bid/accept price environment.

Fasturn quickly migrated into vertical portal services within the apparel industry. Buyers can upload designs, specify order characteristics, search a worldwide factory database, create a purchase order, and track work-in-progress up to and including delivery. Buyers and suppliers also have access to

Exhibit A-3. Trading communities: integrated network.

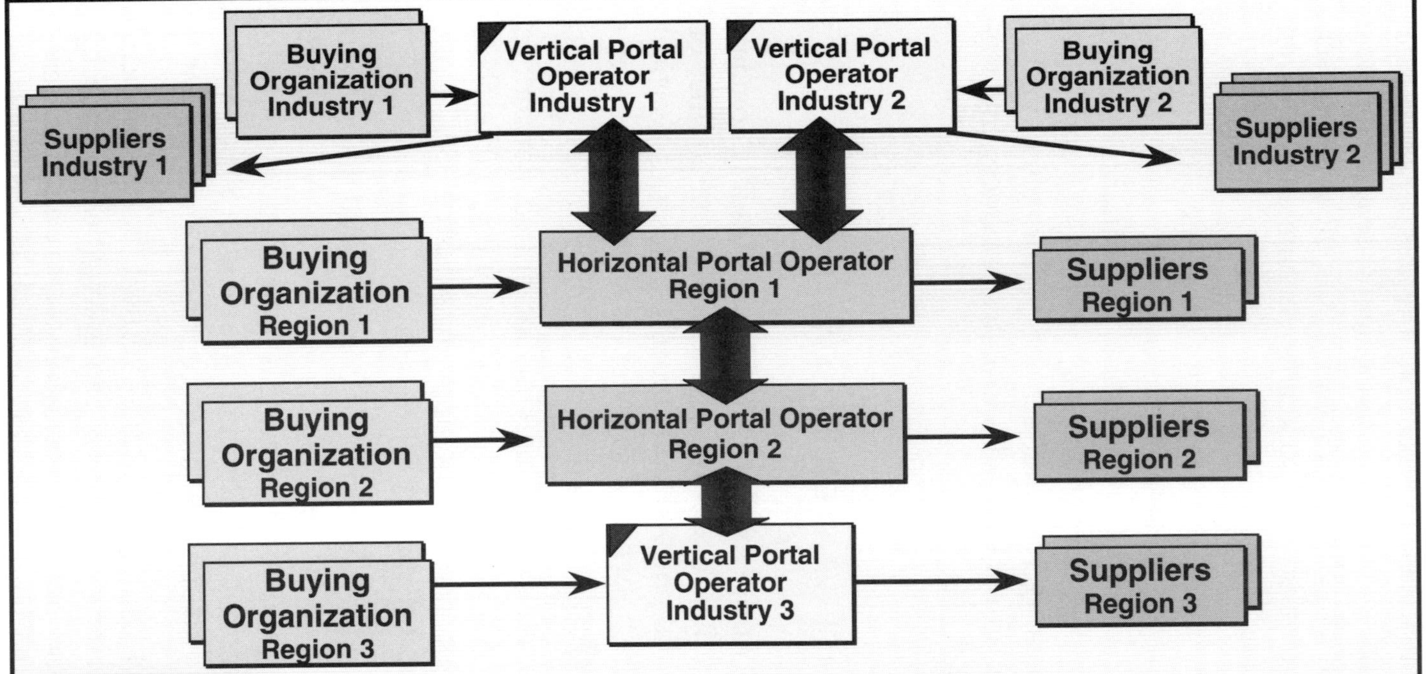

Features:

- Vertical portals tie into the horizontal portal in any region.
- The entire network of suppliers is shared.

Source: Cap Gemini Ernst & Young.

services that include inspection, insurance, logistics, and import/export from the network of Fasturn service partners.[1]An integrated network usually relies on a technology solution like i2's TradeMatrix solution to connect the multiple digital marketplaces or exchanges. In addition, the integrated network is highly dependent on the process model supporting it.

PROCESS MODEL

Let us now consider the process model for trading communities. Consider Exhibit A-4, which outlines the essential players and the flow of information, physical delivery, and cash. The processes will vary depending on the industry and on the particular service offerings of the portal. However, let us follow a typical flow of each of these processes.

Information Flow

The information flow will vary depending on the type of market-making technique that is used. Let us first review the flow for a simple catalog order, and then discuss the differences if other techniques such as dynamic pricing or auctioning are used.

Catalog Order

- The supplier provides catalog and price information to the portal operator who receives this information and standardizes the catalogs. Availability of an online catalog is a basic requirement for any exchange, and, generally, it requires a significant level of work for a selling organization to move its catalog online. Errors that have existed over the years in manual catalogs, such as inconsistent abbreviations, obsolete products, bad pricing information, and poor descriptions have to be corrected before placing the catalog online. After the initial effort

Exhibit A-4. Trading communities: process model.

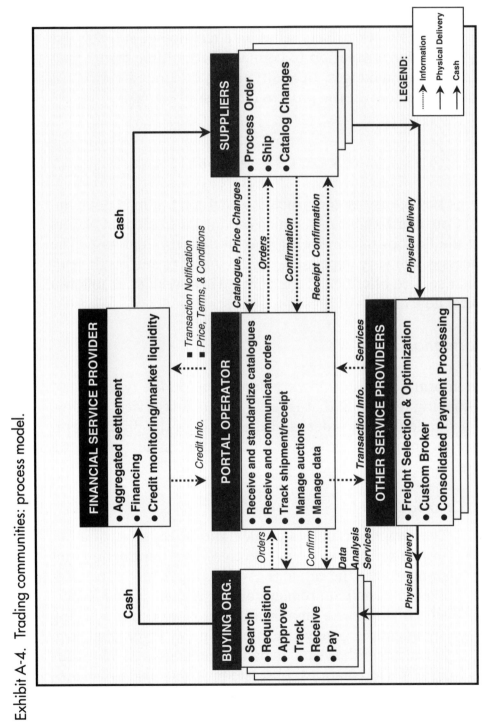

Source: Cap Gemini Ernst & Young.

of moving the catalog online, a significant ongoing maintenance effort is required to insure that the catalog is always accurate and up-to-date regarding product offerings and pricing.

However, there are tools to assist with the creation of an online catalog. Recall that as we discussed in Chapter 2, synchronization of items, pricing, and promotion allowances are not hard with viaLink. The movement of pictorial content (e.g., the JC Penney catalog) is not difficult—just time consuming and somewhat expensive.

⊕ The buying organization searches and reviews the catalog information, and prepares and approves a purchase order, which is sent to the portal operator. Within the buying organization, there is a flow of information to obtain the appropriate levels of approval depending on the value of the purchase order.

⊕ The portal operator receives the order, and communicates it to the supplier.

⊕ The supplier confirms the order, and communicates this information to the portal operator. Ideally, buyers would like to have online product availability information at the time of order placement, but currently that capability is generally not available. The supplier needs to confirm back to the buyer regarding product availability. In fact, in many cases the exchange only matches the buyer and seller, and then leaves actual order fulfillment to be handled offline by the two parties.

⊕ The portal operator passes the order confirmation information to the buying organization.

⊕ After order confirmation, transaction notification goes to the financial services provider. Typically, procurement cards and credit cards are used for the financial transaction.

⊕ Finally, transaction information goes to other service providers such as an LLP handling freight selection, optimization, and a custom broker handling international shipments.

Dynamic Pricing

The information flow varies from above in how buyers and sellers are matched in the ordering process. A prime example of a trade exchange using dynamic pricing is a stock market. Buyers and sellers send buy and sell offers into the exchange at specific prices, and the exchange matches them according to price. This type of exchange is most applicable to commodity-type products with volatile pricing, such as energy and chemicals.

Auctioning

Again, the difference in the information flow is in how buyers and sellers are matched. Auctioning currently represents a very small percentage of trading community activity. It involves unique items with a value that may vary significantly depending on the buyer. The portal operator will manage the bid process for the seller.

Physical Delivery

Whereas in dealing with the flow of information, the portal operator sits in the center of the transaction as the essential facilitator of the information flow, the physical delivery of the product occurs independently of the portal operator. The portal operator does not deal with the physical product. The physical delivery of the product generally occurs similarly to any other purchase transaction. The product is shipped from supplier to buyer typically by common carrier.

Cash Flow

As is the case in physical delivery, the portal operator is generally not involved in the movement of cash from buyer to seller.

Typically, this flow involves the use of a credit card or procurement card, which is similar to a debit card. Therefore, the cash settlement and transaction occurs outside the trade exchange between the buyer, seller, and financial services provider.

VALUE PROPOSITION

Refer again to Exhibit A-4, and let us consider the value proposition for each of the members of the trading community: the buyer organization, the seller organization, the portal operator, and the service providers. What does each have to gain and what is their incentive for participation? In developing a trading community, it is important to establish a win-win situation for all participants in order to have long-term success. There have been situations in the development of trading communities where the sellers have felt pressured to participate, but have not felt that the trading community was to their benefit. From the buyer's perspective, there is significant benefit in combining the spend of numerous organizations and then leveraging that larger spend with the suppliers to obtain greater price discounts. However, from the supplier's perspective, it becomes a "win" for the buyer and a "lose" for the supplier unless the trading community can offer benefits beyond lower prices to the buyer. In a recent value Chain benchmarking study conducted by *Industry Week* magazine in collaboration with Cap Gemini Ernst & Young, pricing pressures were identified as the greatest barrier to value chain optimization.[2] Therefore, the trading community must provide a mechanism to collaborate and share information up and down the value chain, thus creating a win-win situation for all parties involved in the exchange. Now let us examine the benefits to each party in an exchange, which is truly collaborative and beneficial to all.

Buyer Organization

- *Savings in the Cost of Purchased Products and Services.* As discussed above, one of the key advantages for the buying organization is the reduction in price when it purchases products and services. Multiple organizations come together as part of the trading community, and create large volume purchases, which can then be leveraged with suppliers to obtain lower prices.

* *Better Control.* The trading community provides a structure for purchases, which greatly reduces the amount of maverick buying. For companies without a trading community or e-Procurement process, often many people within the organization are buying similar product from multiple vendors at suboptimal prices. The trading community structure creates an organization and supporting technology, which greatly reduces or eliminates that type of buying behavior. Product is purchased through the trading community from the suppliers in the community at the favorable negotiated prices.

* *Standardized Product Specifications.* Often in companies without a trading community or e-Procurement structure, products are designed and specified with significantly more distinct parts than are required. In analyzing the parts usage, one can find multiple parts from multiple vendors being used in situations where a standardized part from one vendor could effectively serve the same purpose. This unnecessary parts proliferation leads to increased working capital, product storage, and administrative expenses, as well as increased purchasing costs because of the small volumes ordered of each individual part. By standardizing parts and vendors through the trading community, these costs are all reduced.

* *Reduced Transaction Costs.* The trading community structure significantly reduces the administrative expense of processing a purchase order.

* *Improved Accuracy.* Because of the increased accuracy of the online catalogs within the trading community, order and pricing accuracy is improved, thus reducing

administrative costs and rework associated with order and billing errors.

- *Reduced Services Provider Cost.* Participation in the trading community provides access to improved rates from service providers, such as transportation service providers. Again, these are due to the volume leverage afforded to the trading community.

- *Demand/Supply Planning Collaboration.* Within the framework of the trading community, there is an opportunity for buyers and sellers to collaboratively plan production and inventory requirements. As we discussed in Chapter 2, trading communities such as TradeMatrix provide an opportunity for buyers and sellers to share information on product demand and production capacities so that each can better plan inventory levels and production.

Seller Organization

- *Reduced Transaction Costs.* As with the buyer, the trading community structure significantly reduces the administrative expense of processing an order.

- *Access to Broader Markets/Increased Sales.* The trading community provides the seller with immediate access to a much broader customer base, thus allowing for opportunities for significant revenue increases. In addition, due to ease of ordering, volume from existing customers is likely to increase.

- *Customer Retention.* Because of the "stickiness" provided by the trading community, the buyer has a tighter link to the supplier, thus improving long-term customer retention.

- *Quicker Order to Cash Process.* The information and transaction flow within the trading community provides a quicker order-to-cash process, thus improving the cash flow of the seller.

- *Improved Order Accuracy.* Orders created online through the online catalog will be significantly more accurate (pricewise, etc.), thereby reducing rework time and time devoted to resolving errors and billing discrepancies.

- *Reduced Service Provider Costs* Participation in the exchange provides volume leverage resulting in reduced costs by service providers.

- *Demand/Supply Planning Collaboration.* As discussed above, a significant advantage of trading communities is the ability of buyers and sellers to collaborate and share information. From the suppliers' perspective, this provides significant benefit in terms of better understanding buyer demand requirements, and thereby adjusting production to meet those demands. Collaboration thus results in reduced inventory levels, fewer backorders or stockouts, and improved production capacity planning.

Portal Operator

There is a variety of different models for operation of the portal itself. In some cases, a consortium of buyers will join to create an exchange, which may be public or private. A prime example of this is the GM/Ford/DaimlerChrylser exchange. In other situations, a dominant supplier may initiate an exchange (e.g., Grainger.com). Thirdly, a market maker may create an exchange supported by venture capital, which is independent of buyers or sellers. In all of these cases, the exchange has a number of revenue opportunities as described here:

- *Buyer/Seller Transaction or Subscription Fees.* An exchange will typically charge a transaction fee ranging from 1 percent to 2 percent for catalog orders. Auction service fees are typically higher. Some exchanges charge an annual subscription fee based on projected volumes.

- *Advertising Fees.* Rates vary depending on the size of the audience.
- *Data Fees.* Statistics regarding activity within the exchange can be collected, aggregated, analyzed, and sold
- *Catalog Fees.* Fees for loading and maintaining product catalogs in the exchange.

Service Providers

Finally, let us consider the benefits to service providers such as transportation providers and financial institutions. In Chapter 6, we discussed many of these benefits in the context of a 3PL or LLP becoming involved in a trading community. These benefits include:

- *Access to Broader Markets.* The exchange provides access to new customers as well as opportunities for additional business and cross selling with existing customers.
- *Reduced Transaction-Processing Fees.*
- *Reduction in Payment Cycle Time.*
- *Freight Consolidation Opportunities.*

SUMMARY

Trading communities can provide a tremendous opportunity for all involved; buyers, sellers, portal operators, and service providers. The collaboration and sharing of infrastructure and information allows tremendous efficiencies to occur throughout the networked supply chain, thus allowing for real costs to be removed from the supply chain. The benefits can be shared throughout the supply chain, thus allowing for a true win-win situation for all involved.

NOTES

1. Fasturn home page: http://www.fasturn.com (Management, pp. 1–3; Services, pp. 1–2; Frequently Asked questions, pp. 1–3; Partners pp. 1–4.

2. "Forging the Chain," *Industry Week* magazine, May 15, 2000, p. 45.

Appendix B

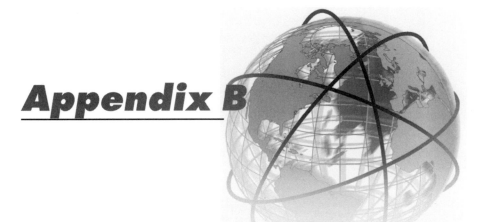

SOURCING / E-PROCUREMENT METHODOLOGY

Appendix A discusses trading communities and their importance in the networked supply chain. Currently, the primary focus of trading communities in the marketplace is in the area of e-Procurement. (Although long-term, we do expect a greater emphasis on activities such as fulfillment and collaborative planning.) We want to emphasis that the e-Procurement function as part of a trading community is but one aspect of a company's sourcing strategy. It is essential that a company consider its entire sourcing strategy before embarking on involvement with e-Procurement within a trading community. Value and savings can only be maximized and sustained through an Internet-enabled e-Procurement solution when it is aligned with an effective sourcing strategy.

During the development of the sourcing strategy, the Sourcing Positioning Quadrant as shown in Exhibit B-1 can be established to guide the sourcing strategy implementation. This quadrant groups the products or materials to be sourced into four main sections. The Y-axis is "Business Impact," and ranges from low to high. The X-axis is "Supply Market Challenges and Cost," and ranges from low to high. The four main sections are as follows:

1. Non-Critical (low business impact, low supply market challenges)
2. Leverage (high business impact, low supply market challenges)
3. Bottleneck (low business impact, high supply market challenges)
4. Strategic (high business impact, high supply market challenges)

Each section carries with it a different sourcing strategy. For the "Noncritical" materials, cost minimization is the top objective. Multiple suppliers in an auction or low-cost bidder environment usually are the method to pursue this objective.

Exhibit B-1. The sourcing positioning quadrant.

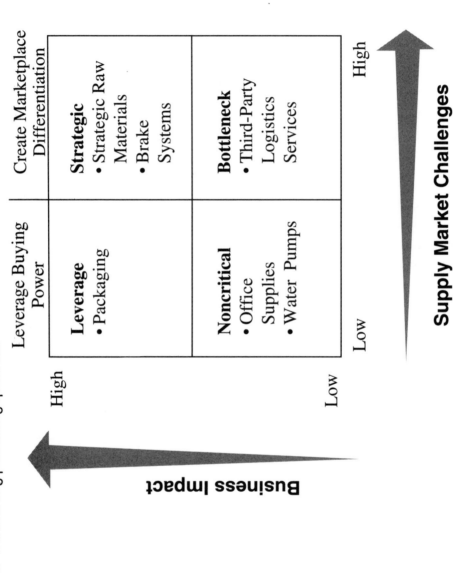

Source: Cap Gemini Ernst & Young.

For the "Leverage" materials, active participation in the value/cost chain of the commodity is the top objective. The trading in futures (e.g., petroleum) by suppliers and buyers to leverage their combined buying power and lower the overall cost of the delivered materials is an example of how to pursue this objective.

For the "Bottleneck" materials, active participation in the networked supply chain to remove the inhibitors to the supply/demand matrix is the top objective. Suppliers in this quadrant usually provide materials that cross global borders, are low to moderate in price, and provide a complex sourcing trade-off between sourcing locally in foreign countries versus from a primary point.

For "Strategic" materials, active pursuit in partnership development of new materials or new processes is the top objective. Frito-Lay works with selected farmers to produce an improved seed potato for chipping potatoes. Automotive OEMs work with brake suppliers to produce the next generation brake systems.

From Quick Wins Implementation through Commodity Sourcing Strategy Development to Commodity Sourcing Strategy Implementation, the sourcing positioning quadrant will govern the categorization of suppliers and the sourcing approach for each supplier.[1]

We would like to thank the Sourcing/E-Procurement practice at Cap Gemini Ernst & Young (CGEY) led by Kevin Poole and the Center for Business Transformation at CGEY for allowing us to share with you a high-level view of the methodology used within CGEY to develop a complete sourcing/e-procurement strategy. Exhibit B-2 shows the high-level phases of the methodology. For each phase, CGEY has developed very detailed stages, activities, and sample work products that must be completed in order to develop an effective sourcing/e-procurement strategy and approach.

Following is a brief description of each of the phases.

Exhibit B-2. Cap Gemini Ernst & Young's sourcing methodology.

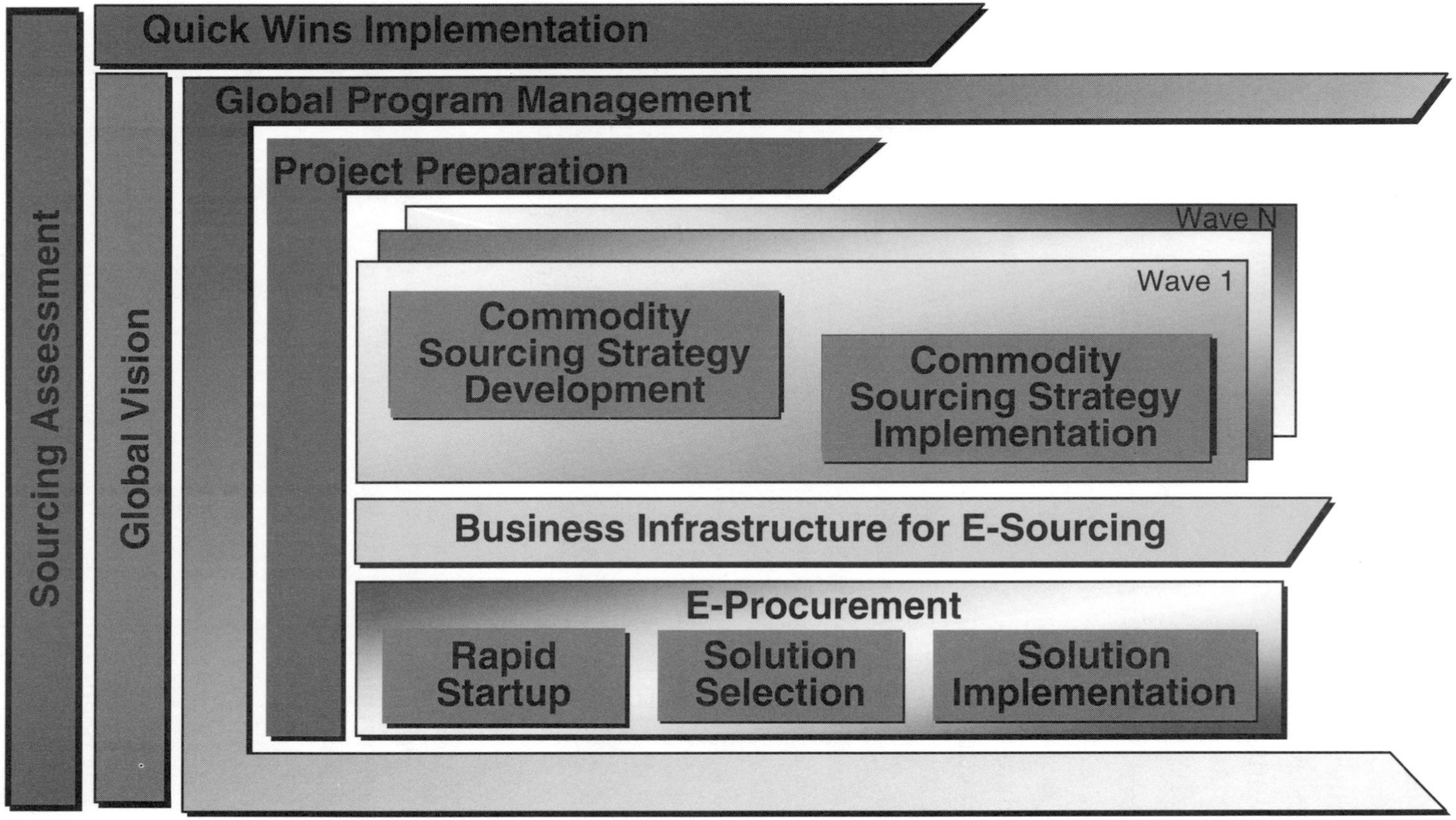

Quick Wins Implementation

Global Program Management

Project Preparation

Wave N

Wave 1

Commodity Sourcing Strategy Development

Commodity Sourcing Strategy Implementation

Business Infrastructure for E-Sourcing

E-Procurement

Rapid Startup

Solution Selection

Solution Implementation

Global Vision

Sourcing Assessment

Source: Cap Gemini Ernst & Young.

- *Sourcing Assessment.* Leveraging Cap Gemini Ernst & Young's Sourcing point of view, the sourcing assessment phase sets out to develop a future state sourcing, operating, and business model, and a high-level implementation plan to build, deploy, implement, and sustain it.

- *Global Vision.* The purpose of this phase is to develop a new global vision that is linked to strategy, organization, process, and technology.

- *Quick Wins Implementation.* The purpose of this phase is to identify, validate, target, plan, and implement a portfolio of improvements that will yield benefits within a three-month window.

- *Global Program Management.* The purpose of this phase is to initiate a management program to track program-wide organizational and project performance. The global program management phase is used to identify and manage project performance and change in a consistent way, and to perform organizational communications, training, and knowledge transfer from a more global perspective.

- *Project Preparation.* The purpose of the Project Preparation phase is to provide initial planning and preparation for each individual project conducted in the Sourcing Methodology. Although each project has its own unique objectives, scope, and priorities, the activities in this phase focus on identifying and planning the primary focus areas to be considered.

- *Commodity Sourcing Strategy Development.* The purpose of this phase is to generate and thoroughly understand a commodity group profile in order to develop a commodity sourcing strategy. An essential component is to understand and integrate current and future business needs into the approach to market.

- *Commodity Sourcing Strategy Implementation.* The purpose of this phase is to provide an approach that encompasses the design of commodity-specific structural changes, the development of work plans to carry out the implementation of the changes, and execution of controls and measures to institutionalize and sustain the improvements put forth in the commodity sourcing strategy.

⊕ *Business Infrastructure for Sourcing.* The purpose of the business infrastructure for e-sourcing is to provide the framework to evaluate and implement a strategic sourcing and/or e-procurement solution. The objective of this phase is to create a design of the future procurement strategy, organization, process, and technology necessary to support the new business.

⊕ *E-Procurement Rapid Startup.* This phase is to be used ONLY when an e-procurement project is conducted as a STAND-ALONE project. All activities covered in this phase are a subset of activities completed in Sourcing Assessment and Global Vision . The objective of the Rapid Start-Up phase is to support an accelerated approach to conducting an e-procurement assessment, identifying improvement opportunities, developing high-level technology, catalogue, content management strategies, and gathering the initial data to support a cost/benefit analysis for an Internet-enabled e-procurement solution selection and implementation.

The CGEY sourcing point of view is that our clients should have implemented an effective, comprehensive sourcing/procurement strategy before considering their e-procurement needs. Value and savings can be maximized and sustained through an Internet-enabled e-procurement solution when it is aligned with a sourcing strategy.

⊕ *E-Procurement Solution Selection.* The purpose of the Solution Selection Phase is to identify the functional and technical requirements for an e-procurement solution; identify, evaluate, and select a technology solution;

refine the solution integration architecture; and build the implementation plan to ensure the successful deployment of an e-procurement solution.

- *E-Procurement Solution Implementation.* The purpose of this phase is to implement an e-procurement solution to accelerate and/or sustain strategic sourcing savings, and to reduce the cost of purchasing nonproduction goods and services through improved controls.

Note

1. Fred A. Kuglin and Barbara A. Rosenbaum, "Logistics" (Chapter 9), in *Guide to Cost Management,* Barry Brinker, editor (New York: John Wiley & Sons, 2000), pp. 146–147.

INDEX